The Cay

and Related Readings

McDougal Littell
A HOUGHTON MIFFLIN COMPANY
Evanston, Illinois • Boston • Dallas

Acknowledgments

Bantam Doubleday Dell Books For Young Readers: *The Cay* by Theodore Taylor. Copyright © 1969 by Theodore Taylor. Published by arrangement with Bantam Doubleday Dell Books For Young Readers, a division of Bantam Doubleday Dell Publishing Group, Inc., New York, New York. All rights reserved.

Alfred A. Knopf, Inc.: "Long Trip," "Sea Calm," and "Death of an Old Seaman," from *Collected Poems* by Langston Hughes. Copyright © 1994 by the Estate of Langston Hughes. Reprinted by permission of Alfred A. Knopf, Inc.

Houghton Mifflin Company: "The Shark," from *Fast and Slow* by John Ciardi. Copyright © 1975 by John Ciardi. Reprinted by permission of Houghton Mifflin Company. All rights reserved.

McIntosh & Otis, Inc.: Excerpt from *The Killer Storms* by Gary Jennings. Copyright © 1970 by Gary Jennings. Reprinted by permission of McIntosh and Otis, Inc.

Continued on page 152

The editors have made every effort to trace the ownership of all copyrighted selections found in this book and to make full acknowledgment for their use. Omissions brought to our attention will be corrected in a subsequent edition.

Cover illustration Copyright © 1997 Pam Rossi.
Background photo: Copyright © Tim Brown/Tony Stone Images.
Author image by John Graves.

Printed in the United States of America.

ISBN 0-395-89330-5

789-QNT-03 02

Contents

The Cay

Theodore Taylor

*To Dr. King's dream, which
can only come true if the
very young know and understand.*

APRIL 1968
LAGUNA BEACH,
CALIFORNIA

Chapter 1

Like silent, hungry sharks that swim in the darkness of the sea, the German submarines arrived in the middle of the night.

I was asleep on the second floor of our narrow, gabled green house in Willemstad, on the island of Curaçao, the largest of the Dutch islands just off the coast of Venezuela. I remember that on that moonless night in February 1942, they attacked the big Lago oil refinery on Aruba, the sister island west of us. Then they blew up six of our small lake tankers, the tubby ones that still bring crude oil from Lake Maracaibo to the refinery, Curaçaosche Petroleum Maatschappij, to be made into gasoline, kerosene, and diesel oil. One German sub was even sighted off Willemstad at dawn.

So when I woke up there was much excitement in the city, which looks like a part of old Holland, except that all the houses are painted in soft colors, pinks and greens and blues, and there are no dikes.

It was very hard to finish my breakfast because I wanted to go to Punda, the business district, the oldest part of town, and then to Fort Amsterdam where I could look out to sea. If there was an enemy U-boat out there, I wanted to see it and join the people in shaking a fist at it.

I was not frightened, just terribly excited. War was something I'd heard a lot about, but had never seen. The whole world was at war, and now it had come to us in the warm, blue Caribbean.

The first thing that my mother said was, "Phillip, the enemy has finally attacked the island, and there will be no school today. But you must stay near home. Do you understand?"

I nodded, but I couldn't imagine that a shell from an enemy submarine would pick me out from all the buildings, or hit me if I was standing on the famous pontoon bridge or among the ships way back in the Schottegat or along St. Anna Bay.

So later in the morning, when she was busy making sure that all our blackout curtains were in place, and filling extra pots with fresh water, and checking our food supply, I stole away down to the old fort with Henrik van Boven, my Dutch friend who was also eleven.

I had played there many times with Henrik and other boys when we were a few years younger, imagining we were defending Willemstad against pirates or even the British. They once stormed the island, I knew, long ago. Or sometimes we'd pretend we were the Dutch going out on raids against Spanish galleons. That had happened too. It was all so real that sometimes we could see the tall masted ships coming over the horizon.

Of course, they were only the tattered-sailed native schooners from Venezuela, Aruba, or Bonaire coming in with bananas, oranges, papayas, melons, and vegetables. But to us, they were always pirates, and we'd shout to the noisy black men aboard them. They'd laugh back and go, "Pow, pow, pow!"

The fort looks as though it came out of a storybook, with gun ports along the high wall that faces the sea. For years, it guarded Willemstad. But this one morning, it did not look like a storybook fort at all. There were real soldiers with rifles and we saw machine guns. Men with binoculars had them trained toward the whitecaps, and everyone was tense. They chased us away, telling us to go home.

Instead, we went down to the Koningin Emma Brug, the famous Queen Emma pontoon bridge, which spans the channel that leads to the huge harbor, the Schottegat. The bridge is built on floats so that it can swing open as ships pass in or out, and it connects Punda with Otrabanda, which means "other side," the other part of the city.

The view from there wasn't as good as from the fort, but curious people were there, too, just looking. Strangely, no ships were moving in the channel. The *veerboots,* the ferry boats that shuttled cars and people back and forth when the bridge was swung open, were tied up and empty. Even the native schooners were quiet against the docks inside the channel. And the black men were not laughing and shouting the way they usually did.

Henrik said, "My father told me there is nothing left of Aruba. They hit Sint Nicolaas, you know."

"Every lake tanker was sunk," I said.

I didn't know if that were true or not, but Henrik had an irritating way of sounding official since his father was connected with the government.

His face was round and he was chubby. His hair was straw-colored and his cheeks were always red. Henrik was very serious about everything he said or did. He looked toward Fort Amsterdam.

He said, "I bet they put big guns up there now."

That was a safe bet.

And I said, "It won't be long until the Navy is here."

Henrik looked at me. "Our Navy?" He meant the Netherlands Navy.

"No," I said. "Ours." Meaning the American Navy, of course. His little Navy was scattered all over after the Germans took Holland.

Henrik said quietly, "Our Navy will come too," and I didn't want to argue with him. Everyone felt bad that Holland had been conquered by the Nazis.

Then an army officer climbed out of a truck and told us all to leave the Queen Emma bridge. He was very stern. He growled, "Don't you know they could shoot a torpedo up here and kill you all?"

I looked out toward the sea again. It was blue and peaceful, and a good breeze churned it up, making lines of whitecaps. White clouds drifted slowly over it. But I couldn't see the usual parade of ships coming toward the harbor; the stubby ones or the massive ones with flags of many nations that steamed slowly up the bay to the Schottegat to load gas and oil.

The sea was empty; there was not even a sail on it. We suddenly became frightened and ran home to the Scharloo section where we lived.

I guess my face was pale when I went into the house because my mother, who was in the kitchen, asked immediately, "Where have you been?"

"Punda," I admitted. "I went with Henrik."

My mother got very upset. She grabbed my shoulder and shook it. "I told you not to go there, Phillip," she said angrily. "We are at war! Don't you understand?"

"We just wanted to see the submarines," I said.

My mother closed her eyes and pulled me up against her thin body. She was like that. One minute, shaking me; the next, holding me.

The radio was on, and a voice said that fifty-six men had died on the lake tankers that were blown up and that the governor of the Netherlands' West Indies had appealed to Washington for help. There was no use in asking Amsterdam. I listened to the sorrowful sound of his voice until my mother's hand switched it to off.

Finally she said, "You'll be safe if you do what we tell you to do. Don't leave the yard again today."

She seemed very nervous. But then she was often nervous. My mother was always afraid I'd fall off the sea wall, or tumble out of a tree, or cut myself with a pocketknife. Henrik's mother wasn't that way. She laughed a lot and said, "Boys, boys, boys."

Late in the afternoon, my father, whose name was also Phillip—Phillip Enright—returned home from the refinery where he was working on the program to increase production of aviation gas. He'd been up since two o'clock, my mother said, and please don't ask him too many questions.

They had phoned him that morning to say that the Germans might attempt to shell the refinery and the oil storage tanks, and that he must report to help fight the fires. I had never seen him so tired, and I didn't ask as many questions as I wanted to.

Until the past year, my father and I had done a lot of things together. Fishing or sailing our small boat, or taking long hikes around Krup Bay or Seroe Male, or just going out into the *koenoekoe,* the countryside, together. He knew a lot about trees and fish and birds. But now he always seemed busy. Even on a Sunday, he'd shake his head and say, "I'm sorry, guy, I have to work."

After he had had his pint of cold Dutch ale (he had one every night in the living room after he came home), I asked, "Will they shoot at us tonight?"

He looked at me gravely and answered, "I don't know, Phillip. They might. I want you and your mother to sleep down here tonight, not on the second floor. I don't think you're in any danger, but it's better to sleep down here."

"How many of them are out there?" I thought they might be like schools of fish. Dozens, maybe. I wanted to be able to tell Henrik exactly what my father knew about the submarines.

He shook his head. "No one knows, Phillip. But there must be three of them around the islands. The attacks were in three different places."

"They came all the way from Germany?"

He nodded. "Or from bases in France," he said, loading his pipe.

"Why can't we go out and fight them?" I asked.

My father laughed sadly and tapped his long forefinger on my chest. "You'd like that, would you? But we have nothing to fight them with, son. We can't go out in motorboats and attack them with rifles."

My mother came in from the kitchen to say, "Stop asking so many silly questions, Phillip. I told you not to do that."

Father looked at her strangely. He had always answered my questions. "He has a right to know. He's involved here, Grace."

My mother looked back at him. "Yes, unfortunately," she said.

My mother, I knew, had not wanted to come to Curaçao in late 1939, but my father had argued that he was needed for the war effort even though the United States was not at war then. Royal Dutch Shell had borrowed him from his American company because he was an expert in refineries and gasoline production. But the moment she saw it, my mother decided she didn't like Curaçao and she often complained about the smell of gas and oil whenever the trade winds died down.

It was very different in Virginia where my father had been in charge of building a new refinery on the banks of the Elizabeth River. We'd lived in a small white house on an acre of land with many trees. My mother often talked about the house and the trees; about the change of seasons and the friends she had there. She said it was nice and safe in Virginia.

My father would answer quietly, "There's no place nice and safe right now."

I remembered the summers with lightning bugs and honeysuckle smells; the cold winters when the fields would all be brown and would crackle under my feet. I didn't remember too much else. I was only seven when we'd moved to the Caribbean.

I guess my mother was homesick for Virginia, where no one talked Dutch, and there was no smell of gas or oil, and there weren't as many black people around.

Now, there was a cold silence between my mother and my father. Lately, it had been happening more and more often. She went back into the kitchen.

I said to him, "Why can't they use aircraft and bomb the submarines?"

He was staring toward the kitchen and didn't hear me. I repeated it.

He sighed. "Oh yes. Same answer, Phillip. There are no fighting aircraft down here. To tell you the truth, we don't have any weapons."

Chapter

We finished dinner just as it was getting dark, and my father went outside to look at our house. He wanted to see if the blackout curtains were working. While my mother and I stood by each window, he called out if he saw the slightest crack of light. By the governor's orders, not a light could shine anywhere on the whole island, he said. Then he went back to the refinery.

I crawled onto the couch downstairs about nine o'clock but I couldn't sleep. I kept thinking about the U-boats off our coast and those lake tankers with barefooted Chinese sailors on board. I guess I was waiting for the U-boats to send a shell toward Willemstad.

Then I began to wonder if the Germans would send soldiers too. About nine-thirty I sneaked out of bed, went to the tool house, and took a hatchet out. I put it under the couch. It was the only thing I could think of to use for fighting the Germans.

It must have been eleven o'clock when my father returned from the refinery to get all the flashlights we had in the house. They talked in low voices, but I could hear them.

Mother said, "It's too dangerous to stay here now."

My father answered, "Grace, you know I can't leave."

She said, "Well, then Phillip and I must go back. We'll go back to Norfolk and wait until the danger is over."

I sat up in bed, unable to believe what I was hearing. My father said, "There's more danger in the trip back, unless you go by air, than there is in staying here. If they do shell us, they won't hit Scharloo."

Mother said sharply, "You know I won't fly. I'd be frightened to death to fly."

"We'll talk about it later." My father sounded miserable. Soon afterward he returned to the refinery again.

I thought about leaving the island, and it saddened me. I loved the old fort, and the schooners, the Ruyterkade market with the noisy chickens and squealing pigs, the black people shouting; I loved the koenoekoe with its giant cactus; the divi-divi trees, their odd branches all on the leeward side of the trunk; the beautiful sandy beach at Westpunt. And I'd miss Henrik van Boven.

I also knew that Henrik and his mother would think us cowardly if we left just because a few German submarines were off Curaçao. I was awake most of the night.

The next morning my father said that the Chinese crews on the lake tankers that shuttled crude oil across the sand bars at Maracaibo had refused to sail without naval escorts. He said the refinery would have to close down within a day, and that meant precious gas and oil could not go to England, or to General Montgomery in the African desert.

For seven days, not a ship moved by the Queen Emma bridge, and there was gloom over Willemstad. The people had been very proud that the little islands of Aruba and Curaçao were now among the most important islands in the world; that victory or defeat depended on them. They were angry with the Chinese crews, and on the third day, my father said that mutiny charges had been placed against them.

"But," he said, "you must understand they are very frightened, and some of the people who are angry with them would not sail the little ships either."

He explained to me what it must feel like to ride the cargoes of crude oil, knowing that a torpedo or shell could turn the whole ship into flames any moment. Even though he wasn't a sailor, he volunteered to help man the lake tankers.

Soon, of course, we might also run out of fresh water. It rains very little in the Dutch West Indies unless there is a hurricane, and water from the few wells has a heavy salt content. The big tankers from the United States or England always carried fresh water to us in ballast, and then it was distilled again so that we could drink it. But now, all the big tankers were being held up in their ports until the submarines could be chased away.

Toward the end of the week, we began to run out of fresh vegetables because the schooner-men were also afraid. Now, my mother talked constantly about the submarines, the lack of water, and the shortage of food. It almost seemed that she was using the war as an excuse to leave Curaçao.

"The ships will be moving again soon," my father said confidently, and he was right.

I think it was February 21 that some of the Chinese sailors agreed to sail to Lake Maracaibo. But on that same day a Norwegian tanker, headed for Willemstad, was torpedoed off Curaçao, and fear again swept over the old city. Without our ships, we were helpless.

Then a day or two later, my father took me into the

Schottegat where they were completing the loading of the S.S. *Empire Tern,* a big British tanker. She had machine guns fore and aft, one of the few armed ships in the harbor.

Although the trade wind was blowing, the smell of gas and oil lay heavy over the Schottegat. Other empty tankers were there, high out of the water, awaiting orders to sail once they had cargoes. The men on them were leaning over the rail watching all the activity on the *Empire Tern.*

I looked on as the thick hoses that were attached to her quivered when the gasoline was pumped into her tanks. The fumes shimmered in the air, and one by one, they "topped" her tanks, loading them right to the brim and securing them for sea. No one said very much. With all that aviation gasoline around, it was dangerous.

Then in the afternoon, we went to Punda and stood near the pontoon bridge as she steamed slowly down St. Anna Bay. Many others had come to watch, too, even the governor, and we all cheered as she passed, setting out on her lonely voyage to England. There, she would help refuel the Royal Air Force.

The sailors on the Empire Tern, which was painted a dull white but had rust streaks all over her, waved back at us and held up their fingers in a V-for-victory sign.

We watched until the pilot boat, having picked up the harbor pilot from the *Empire Tern,* began to race back to Willemstad. Just as we were ready to go, there was an explosion and we looked toward the sea. The *Empire Tern* had vanished in a wall of red flames, and black smoke was beginning to boil into the sky.

Someone screamed, "There it is." We looked off to

one side of the flames, about a mile away, and saw a black shape in the water, very low. It was a German submarine, surfaced now to watch the ship die.

A tug and several small motorboats headed out toward the Tern, but it was useless. Some of the women cried at the sight of her, and I saw men, my father included, with tears in their eyes. It didn't seem possible that only a few hours before I had been standing on her deck. I was no longer excited about the war; I had begun to understand that it meant death and destruction.

That same night, my mother told my father, "I'm taking Phillip back to Norfolk." I knew she'd made up her mind.

He was tired and disheartened over what had happened to the Empire Tern. He did not say much. But I do remember him saying, "Grace, I think you are making a mistake. You are both quite safe here in Scharloo." I wondered why he didn't simply order her to stay. But he wasn't that kind of a man.

The sunny days and dark, still nights passed slowly during March. The ships had begun to sail again, defying the submarines. Some were lost. Henrik and I often went down to Punda to watch them go out, hoping that they would be safe.

Neither my father nor my mother talked very much about us leaving. I thought that when two American destroyers arrived, along with the Dutch cruiser Van Kingsbergen, to protect the lake tankers, Mother would change her mind. But it only made her more nervous.

Then one day in early April, she said, "Your father has finally secured passage for us, so today will be your last day in school here, Phillip. We'll start packing tomorrow, and on Friday, we leave aboard a ship for Miami. Then we'll take the train to Norfok."

Suddenly, I felt hollow inside. Then I became angry and accused her of being a coward. She told me to go off to school. I said I hated her.

All that day in school, I tried to think of what I could do. I thought about going somewhere and hiding until the ship had sailed, but on an island the size of Curaçao, there is no place to hide. Also, I knew it would cause my father trouble.

That night when he got home, I told him I wanted to stay with him. He smiled and put his long, thin arm around my shoulder. He said, "No, Phillip, I think it is best that you go with your mother. At a time like this, I can't be at home very much."

His voice seemed sad, although he was trying to be cheerful. He told me how wonderful it would be to return to the United States; how many things I had missed while we were on the island. I couldn't think of one.

Then I talked to my mother about staying on in Willemstad, and she became very upset with both of us. She said that we didn't love her and began to cry.

My father finally ended it by saying, "Phillip, the decision is made. You'll leave Friday with your mother."

So I packed, with her help, and said good-by to Henrik van Boven and the other boys. I told them we'd be gone just a short time; that we were going to visit my grandparents, my mother's parents, in Norfolk. But I had the feeling that it might be a very long time before I saw Curaçao and my father again.

Early Friday morning, we boarded the S.S. *Hato* in St. Anna Channel. She was a small Dutch freighter with a high bow and stern, and a bridge house in the middle between two well decks. I had seen her often in St. Anna Bay. Usually, she ran between Willemstad, Aruba, and Panama. She had a long stack and always puffed thick, black smoke.

In our cabin, which was on the starboard side and opened out to the boat deck, my father said, "Well, you can rest easy, Phillip. The Germans would never waste a torpedo on this old tub." Yet I saw him looking over the lifeboats. Then he inspected the fire hoses on the boat deck. I knew he was worried.

There were eight other passengers aboard, and they were all saying good-by to their relatives just as we were saying good-by to my father. In the tradition, people brought flowers and wine. It was almost like sailing in the days before the war, they told me.

Father was smiling and very gay but when the *Hato*'s whistle blasted out three times, meaning it was time to go, he said good-by to us between clenched teeth. I clung to him for a long time. Finally, he said, "Take good care of your mother."

I said I would.

We sailed down St. Anna Bay, and the Queen Emma bridge parted for us. Through watery eyes, I saw the fort and the old buildings of Punda and Otrabanda. Native schooners were beating in from the sea.

Then my mother pointed. I saw a tall man standing on the wall of Fort Amsterdam, waving at us. I knew it was my father. I'll never forget that tall, lonely figure standing on the sea wall.

The S.S. *Hato* took her first bite of open sea and began to pitch gently. We turned toward Panama, as we had to make a call there before proceeding to Miami. Down on the well decks, fore and aft, were four massive pumps that had to be delivered to Colón, the port at the Atlantic entrance to the Panama Canal.

I stayed out on deck for a long time, sitting by the lifeboat, looking back at Curaçao, feeling lonely and sad.

Finally my mother said, "Come inside now."

Chapter 3

We were torpedoed at about three o'clock in the morning on April 6, 1942, two days after leaving Panama.

I was thrown from the top bunk and suddenly found myself on my hands and knees on the deck. We could hear the ship's whistle blowing constantly, and there were sounds of metal wrenching and much shouting. The whole ship was shuddering. It felt as though we'd stopped and were dead in the water.

My mother was very calm, not at all like she was at home. She talked quietly while she got dressed, telling me to tie my shoes, and be certain to carry my wool sweater, and to put on my leather jacket. Her hands were not shaking.

She helped me put on my life jacket, then put hers on, saying, "Now, remember everything that we were told about abandoning ship." The officers had held drills every day.

As she was speaking, there was another violent explosion. We were thrown against the cabin door, which the steward had warned us not to lock because it might become jammed. We pushed it open and went out to the boat deck, which was already beginning to tilt.

Everything was bright red, and there were great crackling noises. The entire afterpart of the ship was on fire, and sailors were launching the lifeboat that was on our deck. Steam lines had broken, and the steam was hissing out. Heat from the fire washed over us.

When the lifeboat had been swung out, the captain came down from the bridge. He was a small, wiry white-haired man and was acting the way I'd been told captains should act. He stood by the lifeboat in the fire's glow, very alert, giving orders to the crew. He was carrying a briefcase and a navigation instrument I knew to be a sextant. On the other side of the ship, another lifeboat was being launched.

Near us, two sailors with axes chopped at lines, and two big life rafts plunged toward the water, which looked black except for pools of fire from burning fuel oil.

The captain shouted, "Get a move on! Passengers into the boats!" Tins of lubricating oil in the afterholds had ignited and were exploding, but the ones forward had not been exposed to the fire.

A sailor grabbed my mother's hand and helped her in, and then I felt myself being passed into the hands of a sailor on the boat. The other passengers were helped in, and someone yelled, "Lower away." At that moment, the *Hato* lurched heavily and something happened to the boat falls.

The bow tilted downward, and the next thing I knew we were all in the water. I saw my mother near me and yelled to her. Then something hit me from above.

A long time later (four hours I was told), I opened my eyes to see blue sky above. It moved back and forth, and I could hear the slap of water. I had a terrible pain in my head. I closed my eyes again, thinking maybe I was dreaming. Then a voice said, "Young bahss, how are you feelin'?"

I turned my head.

I saw a huge, very old Negro sitting on the raft near me. He was ugly. His nose was flat and his face was broad; his head was a mass of wiry gray hair. For a moment, I could not figure out where I was or who he was. Then I remembered seeing him working with the deck gang of the *Hato*.

I looked around for my mother, but there was no one else on the raft. Just this huge Negro, myself, and a big black and gray cat that was licking his haunches.

The Negro said, "You 'ad a mos' terrible crack on d'ead, bahss. A strong-back glanc' offen your 'ead, an' I harl you board dis raff."

He crawled over toward me. His face couldn't have been blacker, or his teeth whiter. They made an alabaster trench in his mouth, and his pink-purple lips peeled back over them like the meat of a conch shell. He had a big welt, like a scar, on his left cheek. I knew he was West Indian. I had seen many of them in Willemstad, but he was the biggest one I'd ever seen.

I sat up, asking, "Where are we? Where is my mother?"

The Negro shook his head with a frown. "I true believe your mut-thur is safe an' soun' on a raff like dis. Or mebbe dey harl 'er into d'boat. I true believe dat."

Then he smiled at me, his face becoming less terrifying. "As to our veree location, I mus' guess we are somewhar roun' d'cays, somewhar mebbe fifteen latitude an' eighty long. We should 'ave pass dem til' dat mos' treacherous torpedo split d'veree hull. Two minute downg, at d'mos'."

I looked all around us. There was nothing but blue

sea with occasional patches of orange-brown seaweed. No sight of the *Hato,* or other rafts, or boats. Just the sea and a few birds that wheeled over it. That lonely sea, and the sharp pains in my head, and the knowledge that I was here alone with a black man instead of my mother made me break into tears.

Finally the black man said, looking at me from bloodshot eyes, "Now, young bahss, I mos' feel like dat my own self, Timothy, but 'twould be of no particular use to do dat, eh?" His voice was rich calypso, soft and musical, the words rubbing off like velvet.

I felt a little better, but my head ached fiercely.

He nodded toward the cat. "Dis is Stew, d'cook's cat. He climb on d'raff, an' I 'ad no heart to trow 'im off." Stew was still busy licking. "'E got oi-ll all ovah hisself from d'wattah."

I looked closer at the black man. He was extremely old yet he seemed powerful. Muscles rippled over the ebony of his arms and around his shoulders. His chest was thick and his neck was the size of a small tree trunk. I looked at his hands and feet. The skin was alligatored and cracked, tough from age and walking barefoot on the hot decks of schooners and freighters.

He saw me examining him and said gently, "Put your 'ead back downg, young bahss, an' rest awhile longer. Do not look direct at d'sun. 'Tis too powerful."

I felt seasick and crawled to the side to vomit. He came up beside me, holding my head in his great clamshell hands. It didn't matter, at that moment, that he was black and ugly. He murmured, "Dis be good, dis be good."

When it was over, he helped me back to the center

of the raft, saying, "'Tis mos' natural for you to do dis. 'Tis d'shock o' havin' all dis mos' terrible ting 'appen."

I then watched as he used his powerful arms and hands to rip up boards from the outside edges of the raft. He pounded them back together on cleats, forming two triangles; then he jammed the bases into slots between the raft boards. He stripped off his shirt and his pants, then demanded mine. I don't know what happened to my leather jacket or my sweater. But soon, we had a flimsy shelter from the burning sun.

Crawling under it to sprawl beside me, he said, "We 'ave rare good luck, young bahss. D'wattah kag did not bus' when d'raff was launch, an' we 'ave a few biscuit, some choclade, an' d'matches in d'tin is dry. So we 'ave rare good luck." He grinned at me then.

I was thinking that our luck wasn't so good. I was thinking about my mother on another boat or raft, not knowing I was all right. I was thinking about my father back in Willemstad. It was terrible not to be able to tell him where I was. He'd have boats and planes out within hours.

I guess the big Negro saw the look on my face. He said, "Do not be despair, young bahss. Someone will fin' us. Many schooner go by dis way, an' dis also be d'ship track to Jamaica, an' on."

After a bit, lulled by the bobbing of the raft and by the soft, pleasant sounds of the sea against the oil barrel floats, I went to sleep again. I was very tired and my head still ached. The piece of timber must have struck a glancing blow on the left side.

When I next awakened, it was late afternoon. The sun had edged down and the breeze across us was cool. But I felt very hot and the pain had not gone away. The Negro was sitting with his back toward me, humming something in calypso. His back was a great wall of black flesh, and I saw a cruel scar on one shoulder.

I asked, "What is your name?"

Hearing my voice, he turned with a wide grin. "Ah, you are back wit' me. It 'as been lonesome dese veree hours."

I repeated, "What is your name?"

"My own self? Timothy!"

"Your last name?"

He laughed, "I 'ave but one name. 'Tis Timothy.

"Mine is Phillip Enright, Timothy." My father had always taught me to address anyone I took to be an adult as "mister," but Timothy didn't seem to be a mister. Besides, he was black.

He said, "I knew a Phillip who feesh out of St. Jawn, but an outrageous mahn he was." He laughed deep inside himself.

I asked him for a drink of water.

He nodded agreeably, saying, "D'sun do parch." He lifted a hinged section of the raft flooring and drew out the keg, which was about two feet long. There was a tin cup lashed to it. Careful not to spill a drop, he said, "'Tis best to 'ave only an outrageous smahl amount. Jus' enough to wet d'tongue."

"Why?" I asked. "That is a large keg."

He scanned the barren sea and then looked back at me, his old eyes growing remote. "D'large kag 'ave a way o' losin' its veree size."

"You said we would be picked up soon," I reminded him.

"Ah, yes," he said instantly, "but we mus' be wise 'bout what we 'ave."

I drank the tiny amount of water he'd poured out and asked for more. He regarded me silently a moment, then said, his eyes squinting, "A veree lil' more, young bahss."

My lips were parched and my throat was dry. I wanted a whole cup. "Please fill it up," I said.

Timothy poured only a few drops into the bottom. "That isn't enough," I complained. I felt I could drink three cups of it. But he pressed the wooden stopper firmly back into the keg, ignoring me.

I said, "I must have water, Timothy. I'm very hot."

Without answering, he opened the trap in the raft and secured the keg again. It was then that I began to learn what a stubborn old man he could be. I began to dislike Timothy.

"Young bahss," he said, coming back under the shelter, "mebbe before d'night, a schooner will pass dis way, an' if dat 'appens, you may drink d'whole kag. Mebbe d'schooner will not pass dis way, so we mus' make our wattah last."

I said defiantly, "A schooner will find us. And my father has ships out looking for us."

Without even glancing at me, he answered, "True, young bahss." Then he closed his eyes and would not speak to me any more. He just sprawled out, a mound of silent black flesh.

I couldn't hold the tears back. I'm sure he heard me, but he didn't move a muscle of his face. Neither did he look up when I crawled out from under the shelter to get as far away from him as I could. I stayed on the edge of the raft for a long time, thinking about home and rubbing Stew Cat's back.

Although I hadn't thought so before, I was now beginning to believe that my mother was right. She didn't like them. She didn't like it when Henrik and I would go down to St. Anna Bay and play near the schooners. But it was always fun. The black people would laugh at us and toss us bananas or papayas.

She'd say, when she knew where we'd been, "They are not the same as you, Phillip. They are different and they live differently. That's the way it must be." Henrik, who'd grown up in Curaçao with them, couldn't understand why my mother felt this way.

I yelled over at him, "You're saving all the water for yourself."

I don't think he was asleep, but he didn't answer.

When the sky began to turn a deep blue, Timothy roused himself and looked around. He said, with just an unfriendly glance at me, "If luck be, d'flyin' feesh will flop on d'raff. We can save a few biscuit by eatin' d'feesh. Too, wattah is in d'feesh."

I was hungry but the thought of eating raw fish didn't appeal to me. I said nothing.

Just before dark, they began skimming across the water, their short, winglike fins taking them on flights of twenty or thirty feet, sometimes more.

A large one shot out of the water, skimmed toward us, and then slammed into the raft flooring. Timothy grabbed it, shouting happily. He rapped its head with his knife handle and tossed it beneath the shelter. Soon another came aboard, not so large. Timothy grabbed it, too.

Before total darkness, he had skinned them, deftly cutting meat from their sides. He handed me the two largest pieces. "Eat dem," he ordered.

I shook my head.

He looked at me in the fading light and said softly, "We will 'ave no other food tonight. You bes' eat dem, young bahss." With that, he pressed a piece of the fish against his teeth, sucking at it noisily.

Yes, they were different. They ate raw fish.

I turned away from him, over on my stomach. I thought about Curaçao, warm and safe; about our gabled house in Scharloo, and about my father. Suddenly I blamed my mother because I was on the raft with this stubborn old black man. It was all her fault. She'd wanted to leave the island.

I blurted out, "I wouldn't even be here with you if it wasn't for my mother."

I knew Timothy was staring at me through the darkness when he said, "She started dis terrible wahr, eh, young bahss?" He was a shadowy shape across the raft.

Chapter

Total darkness blotted out the sea, and it became cold and damp. Timothy took the shelter down, and we both pulled our shirts and pants back on. They were stiff from salt and felt clammy. The wind picked up, blowing fine chill spray across the raft. Then the stars came out.

We stayed in the middle of the raft, side by side, as it drifted aimlessly over the sea. Stew Cat rubbed his back against the bottoms of my feet and then curled up down there. I was glad because he was warm.

I was thinking that it was very strange for me, a boy from Virginia, to be lying beside this giant Negro out on the ocean. And I guess maybe Timothy was thinking the same thing.

Once, our bodies touched. We both drew back, but I drew back faster. In Virginia, I knew they'd always lived in their sections of town, and us in ours. A few times, I'd gone down through the shacks of colored town with my father. They sold spicy crabs in one shack, I remember.

I saw them mostly in the summer, down by the river, fishing or swimming naked, but I didn't really know any of them. And in Willemstad, I didn't know them very well either. Henrik van Boven did, though, and he was much easier with them.

I asked, "Timothy, where is your home?"

"St. Thomas," he said. "Charlotte Amalie, on St. Thomas." He added, "'Tis a Virgin Islan'."

"Then you are American," I said. I remembered

from school that we had bought the Virgins from Denmark.

He laughed. "I suppose, young bahss. I nevar gave it much thought. I sail all d'islan's, as well as Venezuela, Colombo, Panama. . . . I jus' nevar gave it much thought I was American."

I said, "Your parents were African, Timothy?"

He laughed, low and soft. "Young bahss, you want me to say I true come from Afre-ca?"

"You say what you want." It was just that Timothy looked very much like the men I'd seen in jungle pictures. Flat nose and heavy lips.

He shook his head. "I 'ave no recollection o' anythin' 'cept dese islan's. 'Tis pure outrageous, but I do not remember anythin' 'bout a place called Afre-ca."

I didn't know if he was telling the truth or not. He looked pure African. I said, "What about your mother?"

Now, there was deep laughter in his voice.

"'Tis even more outrageous I do not remember a fatha or my mut-thur. I was raise by a woman call Hannah Gumbs. . . ."

"Then you are an orphan," I said.

"I guess, young bahss, I guess." He was chuckling to himself, rich and deep.

I looked over toward him, but again, he was just a shadowy shape, a large mound. "How old are you, Timothy?" I asked.

"Dat fact is also veree mysterious. Lil' more dan 'cause d'muscle in my legs b'speakin' to me, complain all d'time. But to be true, I do not know exact."

I was amazed that any man shouldn't know his own age. I was almost certain now that Timothy had indeed come from Africa, but I didn't tell him that. I said, "I'm almost twelve." I wanted him to know I was almost twelve so that he would stop treating me as though I were half that age.

"Dat is a veree important age," Timothy agreed. "Now, you mus' get some natural sleep. Tomorrow might be a veree long day, an' we 'ave much to do."

I laughed. There we were on that bucking raft with nothing to do except watch for schooners or aircraft. "What do we have to do?" I asked.

His eyes groped through the darkness for mine. He came up on his elbows. "Stay alive, young bahss, dat's what we 'ave to do."

Soon, it became very cold and I began shivering. Part of it was coldness, but there was also fear. If the raft tipped over, sharks would slash at us, I knew.

My head was aching violently again. During the day, the pain had been dull, but now it was shooting along both sides of my head. Once, sometime during the early night I felt his horny hand on my forehead. Then he shifted my body, placing it on the other side of him.

He murmured, "Young bahss, d'wind 'as shift. You'll be warmer on dis side."

I was still shivering, and soon he gathered me against him, and Stew Cat came back to be a warm ball against my feet. I could now smell Timothy, tucked up against him. He didn't smell like my father or my mother. Father always smelled of bay rum, the shaving lotion he used, and Mother smelled of some kind of perfume or cologne. Timothy smelled different and strong, like the black men who worked on the decks of the tankers when they were loading. After a while, I didn't mind the smell because Timothy's back was very warm.

The raft plunged on across the light swells

throughout the long night.

I do not think he slept much during the night, but I'd been told that old people didn't sleep much anyway. I woke up when there was a pale band of light to the east, and Timothy said, "You fare well, young bahss? How is d'ead?"

"It still hurts," I admitted.

Timothy said, "A crack on d'ead takes a few days to go 'way." He opened the trap on the raft to pull out the water keg and the tin containing the biscuits, the chocolate squares, and dry matches.

I sat up, feeling dizzy. He allowed me half a cup of water and two hard biscuits, then fed Stew Cat with a wedge of leftover flying fish. We ate in silence as the light crept steadily over the smooth, oily sea. The wind had died and already the sun was beginning to scorch.

Timothy chewed slowly on half a biscuit. "Today, young bahss, a schooner will pass. I'd bet a jum on dat."

"I hope so," I said.

"I do tink we are not too far from Providencia an' San Andrés."

I looked hard at Timothy. "Are they islands?"

He nodded.

I kept looking at him. It seemed there was a film, a haze, separating us. I rubbed my eyes and opened them again. But the haze was still there. I glanced over at the red ball of sun, now clear of the horizon. It seemed dim. I said, "I think there is something wrong with my eyes."

Timothy said, "I warn you! You look direct at d'sun yestiddy."

Yes, that was it! I'd looked at the sun too much.

"Today," Timothy said, "do not eben look at d'wattah. D'glare is bad too."

He went about setting up the triangles for our shelter, and I took off my clothes. After he had draped my pants and shirt, I got under the shelter. The pain in my head was almost unbearable now, and I remember moaning. Timothy tore off a piece of his shirt from the shelter roof, soaked it in fresh water and placed it over my eyes. There was worry in his voice as he talked.

Awhile later, I took the cloth off my eyes and looked up. The inside of our shelter was shadowy and dark, but the pain had begun to go away. "It doesn't hurt as much any more," I said.

"Ah, see, it jus' takes time, young bahss."

I put the cool cloth back over my eyes and went to sleep again. When I woke up, it was night. Yet the air felt hot, and the breeze that came across the raft was warm. I lay there thinking.

"What time is it?" I asked.

"'Bout ten."

"At night?"

There was puzzlement in his voice. "'Tis day."

I put my hand in front of my face. Even in the very blackest night, you can see your own hand. But I could not see mine.

I screamed to Timothy, "I'm blind, I'm blind."

"What?" His voice was a frightened roar.

Then I knew he was bending over me. I felt his breath in my face. He said, "Young bahss, you cannot be blin'." He pulled me roughly from the shelter.

"Look at d'sun," he ordered. His hands pointed my face. I felt the strong warmth against it, but everything was black.

The silence seemed to last forever as he held my face toward the sun. Then a long, shuddering sigh came from his great body. He said, very gently, "Now, young bahss, you mus' lie downg an' rest. What 'as happen will go 'way. 'Tis all natural temporary." But his voice was hollow.

I got down on the hot boards, blinking my eyes again and again, trying to lift the curtain of blackness. I touched them. They did not feel any different. Then I realized that the pain had gone away. It had gone away but left me blind.

I could hear my voice saying, far off, "I don't feel any pain, Timothy. The pain has gone away."

I guess he was trying to think it all out. In a few minutes, he answered, "Once, ovah 'round Barbados, a mahn 'ad an outrageous crack on d'ead when a sailin' boom shift. Dis mahn was blin' too. Tree whole day 'e saw d'night. Den it true went away."

"Do you think that is what will happen to me?"

"I tink dat be true, young bahss," he said.

Then he became very quiet.

After a moment, lying there in darkness, hearing the creak of the raft and feeling its motion, it all hit me. I was blind and we were lost at sea.

I began to crawl, screaming for my mother and my father, but felt his hard hands on my arms. He held me tight and said, low and soft, "Young bahss, young bahss." He kept repeating it.

I'll never forget that first hour of knowing I was blind. I was so frightened that it was hard for me to breathe. It was as if I'd been put inside something that was all dark and I couldn't get out.

I remember that at one point my fear turned to anger. Anger at Timothy for not letting me stay in the water with my mother, and anger at her because I was on the raft. I began hitting him and I remember him saying, "If dat will make you bettah, go 'ead."

After a while, I felt very tired and fell back on the hot boards.

Chapter 5

I guess it was toward noon on the third day aboard the raft that Timothy said tensely, "I 'ear a motah."

"A motah?"

"Sssssh."

I listened. Yes, there was a far-off engine sound coming in faintly above the slap of the sea. Then I could hear Timothy moving around. "'Tis an aircraft," he said.

My heart began to pound. *They were looking for us.* I felt around, then crawled from beneath the shelter to look toward the sound. But I could see nothing.

I heard the hinges on the trap door creak. Timothy said quietly, as though afraid to chase the sound away, "It knowin' what we doin' 'ere by seein' smoke, I do believe."

He ripped down one of the triangle legs, and I heard cloth tearing. Soon he said, "We made d' torch, young bahss. D' mahn up dere be seein' d'smoke all right, all right."

The faint drone of the aircraft seemed closer now. In a moment, I smelled cloth burning and knew he was holding the wrapped piece of wood toward the sky.

He shouted, "Look downg 'ere."

But already the drone seemed to be fading.

Timothy yelled, "I see it, I see it! Way to port!"

I tried to make my eyes cut through the darkness. "Is he coming our way?"

"Don' know, don' know, young bahss," Timothy replied anxiously.

I said, "I can't hear it now." There was nothing in the air but the sea sounds.

Timothy shouted, "Look downg 'ere! Dere is a raff wit a lil' blin' boy, an' old mahn, an' Stew Cat. Look downg 'ere, I tell you."

The drone could not be heard. Just the slap of the water and the sound of the light wind making our shelter flap.

We were alone again on the ocean.

After a moment of silence, I heard the sizzle of the water as Timothy doused the torch. He sighed deeply, "I be ready next time for true. Let d'torch dry, den I be ready."

Soon he sat down beside me. "'Tis a good ting not to harass d'soul ovah dis. We are edgin' into d'aircraft track, same as d'ship dey run."

I said nothing but put my head down on my knees.

"Do not be dishearten, young bahss. Today, we will be foun', to be true."

But the long, hot day was passing without sight of anything. I knew Timothy was constantly scanning the sea. It was all so calm now that the raft didn't even seem to be drifting. Once, I crawled over to the edge to touch the warm water and felt Timothy right behind me.

He said, "Careful, young bahss. D'sharks always hungry, always waitin' for d'mahn to fall ovahboard."

Drawing back from the edge, I asked, "Are there many here?"

"Yes, many 'ere. But long as we 'ave our raff, they do not meliss us."

Standing on the sea wall at Willemstad, sometimes

I'd seen their fins in the water. I'd also seen them on the dock at the Ruyterkade market, their mouths open and those sharp teeth grinning.

I went back under the shelter, spending a long time rubbing Stew Cat. He purred and pushed himself along my body. I was glad that I had seen him and had seen Timothy before going blind. I thought how awful it would have been to awaken on the raft and not know what they looked like.

Timothy must have been standing over us, for he said, "D'cot not good luck." After a moment he added, "But to cause d'death of a cot is veree bad luck."

"I don't think Stew Cat is bad luck," I said. "I'm glad he is here with us."

Timothy did not answer, but turned back, I guess, to watch the sea again. I could imagine those bloodshot eyes, set in that massive, scarred black face, sweeping over the sea.

"Tell me what's out there, Timothy," I said. It was very important to know that now. I wanted to know everything that was out there.

He laughed. "Jus' miles o' blue wattah, miles o' blue wattah."

"Nothing else?"

He realized what I meant. "Oh, to be sure, young bahss, I see a feesh jump way fo'ward. Dat mean large feesh chase 'im. Den awhile back, a turtle pass us port side, but too far out to reach 'im back. . . ."

His eyes were becoming mine. "What's in the sky, Timothy?"

"In d'sky?" He searched it. "No clouds, young bahss, jus' blue like 'twas yestiddy. But now an' den, I see a petrel. While ago, a booby . . ."

I laughed for the first time all day. It was a funny name for a bird. "A booby?"

Timothy was quite serious. "Dis booby I saw was a blue face, mebbe nestin' out o' Serranilla Bank, mebbe not. Dey be feedin' on d'flyin' feesh. I true watchin' d'birds 'cause dey tell us we veree close to d'shore."

"How does a booby look, Timothy?"

"Nothin' much," he replied. "Tail like our choclade, sharp beak, mos' white on 'is body."

I tried to picture it, wondering if I'd ever see a bird again.

Chapter

In the early morning (I knew it was early because the air was still cool and there was dampness on the boards of the raft), I heard Timothy shout, "I see an islan', true."

In wild excitement, I stumbled up and fell overboard.

I went under the water, yelling for him, then came up, gasping. I heard a splash and knew he was in the water too.

Something slapped up against my leg, and I thought it was Timothy. I knew how to swim, but didn't know which way to go. So I was treading water. Then I heard Timothy's frightened roar, "Sharks," and he was thrashing about near me.

He grabbed my hair with one hand and used his other arm to drag me back toward the raft. I had turned on my face and was trying to hold my breath. Then I felt my body being thrown, and I was back on the boards of the raft, gasping for air. I knew that Timothy was still in the water because I could hear splashing and cursing.

The raft tilted down suddenly on one side. Timothy was back aboard. Panting, he bent over me. He yelled, "Damn fool mahn! I tol' you 'bout d'shark!"

I knew Timothy was in a rage. I could hear his heavy breathing and knew he was staring at me. "Shark all 'round us, all d'time," he roared.

I said, "I'm sorry."

Timothy said, "On dis raff, you crawl, young bahss. You 'ear me?"

I nodded. His voice was thick with anger, but in a moment, after he took several deep breaths, he asked, "You all right, young bahss?"

I guess he sat down beside me to rest. His breathing was still heavy. Finally, he said, "Mahn die quick out dere."

We'd both forgotten about the island. I said, "Timothy, you saw an island!"

He laughed. "Yes, d'islan'! Dere 'tis. . . ."

I said, "Where?"

Timothy answered scornfully, "Dere, look, mahn, look . . ."

Angrily, I said to him, "I can't see." He kept forgetting that.

His voice was low when he said, "Yes, young bahss. Dat be true! In all dis harassment wid d'shark, I did forget."

Then I felt his hands on my shoulders. He twisted them. "Dat direction, young bahss."

Straining to look where he had me pointed, I asked, "Are there any people on it?"

"'Tis a veree smahl islan', outrageous low."

I repeated, "Are there any people on it?" I thought they could contact my father and then send for help.

Timothy answered honestly, "No, young bahss. No people. People not be libin' on d'islan' dat 'as no wattah."

No people. No water. No food. No phones. It was not any better than the raft. In fact, it might be worse. "How far away are we?"

"'Bout two mile," Timothy said.

"Maybe we should stay on the raft. A schooner will see us, or an airplane."

Timothy said positively, "No, we bettah off on lan'. An' we driftin' dat way. D'tide be runnin' wid us." His voice was happy. He wanted to be off the sea.

I was certain my father had planes and ships out looking for us. I said, "Timothy, the Navy is searching for us. I know."

Timothy did not answer me. He just said, "'Tis a pretty ting, to be sure. I see a white beach, an' behin' dat, low sea-grape bushes; den on d'hill, some palm. Mebbe twenty, thirty palm."

I was sure he couldn't even see that far.

I said, "Timothy, wouldn't it be better if we stayed on the raft and found a big island with people on it?"

He ignored me. He said, "Bidin' d'night, I saw surf washin' white ovah banks off to port, but did not awaken you, young bahss. But knew we be gettin, near d'cays. . . ."

I said, "I don't want to go on that island."

I don't think there was anyone on earth as stubborn as old Timothy. There was steel in his voice when he answered, "We be goin' on dat islan', young bahss. Dat be true."

But he knew how I felt now, because he added, "From dis islan', we will get help. Be true, I swear. . . ."

Chapter 7

It seemed hours but it was probably only one until Timothy said, "Do not be alarm now, young bahss. I am goin' to jump into d'wattah an' kick dis raff to d'shore. Widout dat, we'll pass d'islan', by-'n'-by."

In a moment, I heard a splash on one side of the raft and then Timothy's feet began drumming the water. I guess he was not afraid of sharks this close in. Soon, he yelled, "Boddam, young bahss, boddam." His feet had touched sand. In another few minutes, the raft lurched and I knew it had grounded.

I listened for sounds from shore, hoping there would be a cheerful "hello," but there were none. Just the wash of the low surf around the raft.

Timothy said, "'Ere, young bahss, on my shoulders an' I'll fetch you to d'lan'." He helped me to his back.

I said, "Don't forget Stew Cat."

He laughed back heartily. "One at a time, young bahss."

With me on his back, he splashed ashore, and judging from the time it took, the raft wasn't very far out. Then he lifted me down again.

"Lan'," he shouted.

The warm sand did feel good on my feet, and now I was almost glad that we wouldn't have to spend another night on the hard, wet boards of the raft.

He said, "Touch it, young bahss. Feel d'lan', 'tis outrageous good."

I reached down. The grains of sand felt very fine, almost like powder.

Timothy said, "'Tis a beautiful cay, dis cay. Nevah hab I seen dis cay." Then he led me to sit under a clump of bushes. He said, "You res' easy while I pull d'raff more out of d'wattah. We mus' not lose it."

I sat there in the shade, running sand through my fingers, wondering where, among all those many islands in the Caribbean, we were.

Timothy shouted up from the water, "Many feesh 'ere. *Langosta,* too, I b'knowin'. We ros' dem."

Langosta, I knew, was the native lobster, the one without claws. I heard Timothy splashing around down by the surf and knew he was pulling the raft up as far as he could get it.

A moment later, puffing hard, he flopped down beside me. He said, "Cotch me breath, den I will tour d'islan', an' select a place for d'camp. . . ."

He put Stew Cat into my lap.

"Camp?" I asked, stroking big Stew.

Timothy replied, "We mebbe 'ere two, tree days. So we be libin' comfortable."

He could tell I was discouraged because we had come to the island and there were no people on it. He said confidently, "We be rescue, true. Before d'night, I build a great fire pile o' brush an' wood. So d'nex' aircraft dat fly ovah, we set it off."

"Where are we, Timothy? Near Panama?"

He answered slowly, "I cannot be sure, young bahss. Not veree sure."

"But you said you knew about the banks and the cays that are near the banks." I wondered if he knew anything, really, or if he was just a stupid old black man.

Timothy said, "Lissen, I know dat many banks an' cays are roun' fifteen north an' eighty long. Dere is Roncador an' Serranno; Quito Sueño an' Serranilla an' Rosalind; den dere is Beacon an' North Cay. Off to d'wes', somewhere, is Providencia an' San Andrés . . ." He paused a moment and then said, "Far 'way, up dere, I tink, is d'Caymens, an' den Jamaica."

"But you are not sure of this island?"

Timothy answered gravely, "True, I am not sure."

"Do the schooners usually come close by here?" I asked.

Again very gravely, Timothy said, "D'mahn who feeshes follows d'feesh. Sartainly, d'feesh be 'ere. I be seein' wid my own self eyes."

I kept feeling that Timothy was holding something back from me. It was the tone of his voice. I'd heard my father talk that way a few times. Once, when he didn't want to tell me my grandfather was about to die; another time was when a car ran over my dog in Virginia.

Of course, both times happened when I was younger. Now, my father was always honest with me, I thought, because he said that in the end that was better. I wished Timothy would be honest with me.

Instead he got up to take a walk around the cay, saying he'd be back in a few minutes. Then Stew Cat wandered away. I called to him but he seemed to be exploring too. Realizing that I was alone on the beach I became frightened.

I knew how helpless I was without Timothy. First I began calling for Stew Cat but when he didn't return I began shouting for Timothy. There was no answer. I wondered if he'd fallen down and was hurt. I began to crawl along the beach and ran head on into a clump of low hanging brush.

I sat down again, batting at gnats that were buzzing around my face. Something brushed against my arm, and I yelled out in terror. But I heard a meow and knew it was only Stew Cat. I reached for him and held him tight until I heard brush crackling and sang out, "Timothy?"

"Yes, young bahss," he called back from quite a distance.

When he was closer, I said harshly, "Never leave me again. Don't you ever leave me again!"

He laughed. "Dere is nothin' to fear 'ere. I walked roun' d'whole islan', an' dere is nothin' but sea grape, sand, a few lil' lizzard, an' dose palm tree . . ."

I repeated, "Never leave me alone, Timothy."

"All right, young bahss, I promise," he said.

He must have been looking all around, for he said, "No wattah 'ere, but 'tis no problem. We still 'ave wattah in d'kag, an' we will trap more on d'firs' rain."

Still believing he wasn't telling me everything, I said, "You were gone a long time."

He answered uneasily, "Thirty minutes at mos'. D'islan' is 'bout one mile long, an' a half wide, shaped like d'melon. I foun' a place to make our camp, up near d'palm. 'Twill be a good place for a lookout. D'rise is 'bout forty feet from d'sea."

I nodded, then said, "I'm hungry, Timothy."

We were both hungry. He went back to the raft, took out the keg of water and the tin of biscuits and chocolate.

While we were eating, I said, "You are worried about something, Timothy. Please tell me the truth. I'm old enough to know."

Timothy waited a long time before answering, probably trying to choose the right words. Finally, he said, "Young bahss, dere is, in dis part of d'sea, a few lil' cays like dis one, surround on bot' sides by hombug banks. Dey are cut off from d'res' o' d'sea by dese banks. . . ."

I tried to make a mental picture of that. Several small islands tucked up inside great banks of coral that made navigation dangerous was what I finally decided on.

"You think we are on one of those cays?"

"Mebbe, young bahss, mebbe."

Fear coming back to me—I knew he'd made a mistake in bringing us ashore—I said, "Then no ships will pass even close to us. Not even schooners! We're trapped here!" We might live here forever, I thought.

Again he did not answer directly. I was beginning to learn that he had a way of being honest while still being dishonest. He said, "D'place I am tinking of is call Debil's Mout'. 'Tis a U-shaped ting, wit dese sharp coral banks on either side, runnin' maybe forty, fifty mile. . . ."

He let that sink in. It sounded bad. But then he said, "I do hope, young bahss, dat I am outrageous mistaken."

"If we are in the Devil's Mouth, how can we be rescued?" I asked angrily. It was his fault we were there.

"D'fire pile! When aircraft fly above, dey will see d'smoke an' fire!"

"But they might just think it is a native fisherman. No one else would come here!"

I could picture him nodding, thinking about that. Finally, he said, "True, but we cannot fret 'bout it, can we? We'll make camp, an' see what 'appens."

He poured me a half cup of water, saying happily, "Since we 'ave made lan', we can celebrate."

I drank it slowly and thoughtfully.

Chapter

During the afternoon, Timothy was busy and we did not talk much. He was making a hut of dried palm fronds. I sat near him under a palm. Now that we were on shore, I again began to think about what had happened to my mother. Somehow, I felt she was safe. I was also sure that a search had been started for us, not fully understanding that a war was on and that all the ships and aircraft were needed to fight the U-boats. I even thought about Henrik van Boven and what a story I would have to tell when I saw him again.

I tried not to think about my eyes, sitting there under the palm, listening to Timothy hum as he made the camp. I trusted him that my sight would return within a few days. I also trusted him that an aircraft would spot our fire pile.

In late afternoon, he said proudly, "Look, our hut!"

I had to remind him again, stupid old man, that I couldn't see, so he took my hands and ran them over the fronds. It was a hut, he said, about eight feet wide and six feet deep, with supports made of wood he'd picked off the beach. The supports were tied together with strong vines that covered the north end of the island.

The roof, which sloped back, he said, was about six feet off the ground. I could easily stand up in it, but Timothy couldn't. Not quite.

Timothy said, "Tomorrow, we be gettin' mats to

sleep on, weave our own, but tonight we mus' sleep on d'sand. 'Tis soft."

I knew he was very proud of the hut. It had taken him only a few hours to build it.

"Now," he said, "I mus' go downg to d'reef an' fetch langosta. We'll ros' it, to be true."

I became frightened again the minute he said it. I didn't want to be left alone, and I was afraid something might happen to him. "Take me with you, Timothy," I pleaded.

"Not on d'reef," he answered firmly. "I 'ave not been dere before. If 'tis safe, tomorrow I will take you." With that, he went down the hill without saying another word.

My mother was right, I thought. They had their place and we had ours. He did not really like me, or he would have taken me along. He was different.

It seemed as though he were gone for a very long time. Once, I thought I heard an aircraft, but it was probably just my imagination. I began yelling for Timothy to come back, but I guess he couldn't hear because of water noise on the reef.

The palm fronds above me rattled in the breeze, and there were other noises from the underbrush. I knew Stew Cat was around somewhere, but it didn't sound like him.

I wondered if Timothy had checked for snakes. There were also scorpions on most Caribbean islands, and they were deadly. I wondered if there were any on our cay.

During those first few days on the island, the times I spent alone were terrible. It was, of course, being unable to see that made all the sounds so frightening. I guess if you are born blind, it is not so bad. You grow up knowing each sound and what it means.

Suddenly, the tears came out. I knew it was not a manly thing to do, something my father would have frowned on, but I couldn't stop. Then from nowhere came Stew Cat. He rubbed along my arms and up against my cheek, purring hard. I held him close.

Soon, Timothy came up the hill, shouting, "Young bahss, tree nice langosta."

I refused to speak to him because he had left me for such a long time.

He stood over me and said, "'Ere, touch dem, dey are still alive." He was almost crowing over his lobster.

I turned away. Sooner or later, Timothy would have to understand that he could not ignore me one minute and then treat me as a friend the next.

He said softly, "Young bahss, be an outrageous mahn if you like, but 'ere I'm all you got."

I didn't answer.

He roasted the langosta over the fire, and later we crawled into the hut to spend our first night on the silent island.

Timothy seemed very tired and groaned a lot. Before we went to sleep, I asked him, "Tell me the truth, Timothy, how old are you?"

He sighed deeply, "More dan seventy. Eben more dan seventy. . . ."

He was very old. Old enough to die there.

In the morning, Timothy began making the fire pile down on the beach. He had a plan. We'd always keep a small fire smoldering up by the hut, and if an airplane came near, he'd take a piece of burning wood from our small fire to ignite the big one. That way, he said, we could save the few matches that we had.

It didn't take him long to stack driftwood over dried palm fronds. Then he said, "Now, young bahss, we mus' say somethin' on d'san'."

Sometimes it was difficult to understand Timothy. The soft and beautiful West Indian accent and way of speaking weren't always clear.

"Say something on the sand?" I asked.

"So dey be knowin' we are downg 'ere," he explained patiently.

"Who?"

"D'mahn in d'sky, of course."

"Oh." Now I understood.

I guess Timothy was standing there looking at me, waiting for me to say something or do something. I heard him say, "Well, young bahss."

"What do we do now?" I asked.

His voice now impatient, he said, "Say somethin' wid d'rock, wid many rock; eeevery rock be sayin' somethin'. . . ."

I frowned at him. "I don't think I can help you, Timothy. I can't see any rocks."

Timothy groaned. "I can see d'rock, young bahss. But what do we say?"

I laughed at him, enjoying it now. "We say 'help.'"

He grunted satisfaction.

For the next twenty or thirty minutes, I could hear Timothy dropping rocks against each other, singing softly to himself in calypso. It was a song about "fungee an' feesh." I'd had "fungi" in Willemstad down in the blacks' market at Ruyterkade. It was just plain old corn meal. But most food has different names in the islands.

Soon, he came to stand over me. "Now, young bahss," he said. He seemed to be waiting.

"Yes?"

There was a silence until Timothy broke it with anguish. "Wid d'rock, say 'help.'"

I looked up in his direction and suddenly understood that Timothy could not spell. He was just too stubborn, or too proud, to admit it.

I nodded and began feeling around the sand for a stick.

He asked, "What you reachin' for?"

"A stick to make lines with."

He placed one in my hands, and I carefully lettered H-E-L-P on the sand while he stood above me, watching. He kept murmuring, "Ah-huh, ah-huh," as if making sure I was spelling it correctly.

When I had finished, Timothy said approvingly, "I tell you, young bahss, dat do say help." Then he happily arranged the rocks on the sand, following my lines.

I felt good. I knew how to do something that Timothy couldn't do. *He couldn't spell.* I felt superior to Timothy that day, but I let him play his little game, pretending not to know that he really couldn't spell.

Chapter 9

In the Afternoon, Timothy said we'd make a rope.

On the north end of the island, tough vines, almost as large as a pencil, were laced over the sand. It took us several hours to tear out a big pile of them. Then Timothy began weaving a rope that would stretch all the way down the hill to the beach and fire pile.

The rope was for me. If he happened to be out on the reef, and I heard a plane, I could take a light from our campfire, follow the rope down, and touch off the big fire. The vine rope would also serve to get me safely down to the beach.

After we'd torn the vines out, and he was weaving the rope, he said, "Young bahss, you mus' begin to help wid d'udder wark."

We were sitting up by the hut. I had my back to a palm and was thinking that back in Willemstad, at this moment, I'd probably be sitting in a classroom, three desks away from Henrik, listening to Herr Jonckheer talk about European history. I'd been tutored in Dutch the first year in Willemstad so I could attend the regular school. Now I could speak it and understand it.

My hands were tired from pulling the vines, and I just wanted to sit and think. I didn't want to work. I said, "Timothy, I'm blind. I can't see to work."

I heard him cutting something with his sharp knife. He replied softly, "D'han' is not blin'."

Didn't the old man understand? To work, aside from pulling up vines or drawing something in the sand, you must be able to see.

Stubbornly, he said, "Young bahss, we need sleepin' mats. You can make d'mats."

I looked over in his direction. "You do it," I said.

He sighed back, saying, "D'best matmaker in Charlotte Amalie, downg in Frenchtown, b'total blin'."

"But he's a man, and he has to do that to make a living."

"B'true," Timothy said quietly.

But in a few minutes, he placed several lengths of palm fiber across my lap. He really was a black mule. "D'palm mat is veree easy. Jus' ovah an' under . . ."

Becoming angry with him, I said, "I tell you, I can't see."

He paid no attention to me. "Take dis' han' hol' d'palm like dis; den ovah an' under, like d'mahn in Frenchtown; den more palm."

I could feel him standing there watching me as I tried to reeve the lengths, but I knew they weren't fitting together. He said, "Like dis, I tell you," and reached down to guide my hand. "Ovah an' under . . ."

I tried again, but it didn't work. I stood up, threw the palm fibers at him, and screamed, "You ugly black man! I won't do it! You're stupid, you can't even spell . . ."

Timothy's heavy hand struck my face sharply.

Stunned, I touched my face where he'd hit me. Then I turned away from where I thought he was. My cheek stung, but I wouldn't let him see me with tears in my eyes.

I heard him saying very gently, "B'gettin' back to wark, my own self."

I sat down again.

He began to sing that "fungee and feesh" song in a

low voice, and I could picture him sitting on the sand in front of the hut; that tangled gray hair, the ugly black face with the thick lips, those great horny hands winding the strands of vine.

The rope, I thought. It wasn't for him. It was for me.

After a while, I said, "Timothy . . ."

He did not answer, but walked over to me, pressing more palm fronds into my hands. He murmured, "'Tis veree easy, ovah an' under . . ." Then he went back to singing about fungee and feesh.

Something happened to me that day on the cay. I'm not quite sure what it was even now, but I had begun to change.

I said to Timothy, "I want to be your friend."

He said softly, "Young bahss, you 'ave always been my friend."

I said, "Can you call me Phillip instead of young boss?"

"Phill-eep," he said warmly.

Chapter 10

During our seventh night on the island, it rained. It was one of those tropical storms that comes up swiftly without warning. We were asleep on the palm mats that I'd made, but it awakened us immediately. The rain sounded like bullets hitting on the dried palm frond roof. We ran out into it, shouting and letting the fresh water hit our bodies. It was cool and felt good.

Timothy yelled that his catchment was working. He had taken more boards from the top of the raft and had made a large trough that would catch the rain. He'd picked up bamboo lengths on the beach and had fitted them together into a short pipe to funnel the rain water into our ten-gallon keg.

It rained for almost two hours, and Timothy was quite angry with himself for not making a second catchment because the keg was soon filled and overflowing.

We stayed out in the cool rain for twenty or thirty minutes and then went back inside. The roof leaked badly but we didn't mind. We got on our mats and opened our mouths to the sweet, fresh water. Stew Cat was huddled in a miserable ball over in a corner, Timothy said, not enjoying it at all.

I liked the rain because it was something I could hear and feel; not something I must see. It peppered in bursts against the frond roof, and I could hear the drips as it leaked through. The squall wind was in the tops of the palms and I could imagine how they looked in the night sky, thrashing against each other high over our little cay.

I wanted it to rain all night.

We talked for a long time when the rain began to slack off. Timothy asked me about my mother and father. I told him all about them and about how we lived in Scharloo, getting very lonesome and homesick while I was telling him. He kept saying, "Ah, dat be true?"

Then Timothy told me what he could remember from his own childhood. It wasn't at all like mine. He'd never gone to school, and was working on a fishing boat by the time he was ten. It almost seemed the only fun he had was once a year at carnival when he'd put frangipani leaves around hs ankles and dress up in a donkey hide to parade around with *mocki jumbis,* the spirit chasers, while the old ladies of Charlotte Amalie danced the *bambola* around them.

He chuckled. "I drink plenty rhum dose tree days of carnival."

I could picture him in his donkey skin, wheeling around to the music of the steel bands. They had them in Willemstad too.

Because it had been on my mind I told him that my mother didn't like black people and asked him why.

He answered slowly, "I don' like some white people my own self, but 'twould be outrageous if I didn' like any o' dem."

Wanting to hear it from Timothy, I asked him why there were different colors of skin, white and black, brown and red, and he laughed back, "Why b'feesh different color, or flower b'different color? I true don' know, Phill-eep, but I true tink beneath d'skin is all d'same."

Herr Jonckheer had said something like that in school but it did not mean quite as much as when Timothy said it.

Long after he'd begun to snore in the dripping hut, I thought about it. Suddenly, I wished my father and mother could see us there together on the little island.

I moved close to Timothy's big body before I went to sleep. I remember smiling in the darkness. He felt neither white nor black.

In the morning, the air was crisp and the cay smelled fresh and clean. Timothy cooked a small fish, a pompano, that he'd speared at dawn down on the reef. Neither of us had felt so good or so clean since we had been aboard the *Hato*. And without discussing it, we both thought this might be the day an aircraft would swing up into the Devil's Mouth, if that's where we were.

The pompano, broiled over the low fire, tasted good. Of course, we were eating little but what came from the sea. Fish, langosta, mussels, or the eggs from sea urchins, those small, black round sea animals with sharp spines that attach themselves to the reefs.

Timothy had tried to make a stew from seaweed but it tasted bitter. Then he'd tried to boil some new sea-grape roots but they made us ill. The only thing that ever worked for him was sea-grape leaves, boiled first in sea water and then cooked in fresh water.

But above us, forty feet from the ground, Timothy said, was a feast. Big, fat green coconuts. When we'd landed, there were a few dried ones on the ground, but the meat in them was not very tasty. In a fresher one, there was still some milk, but it was rancid.

At least once a day, especially when we were around the hut, Timothy would say, "'Tis outrageous dem coconut hang up in d'sky when we could use d'milk an' meat." Or he'd say, "Timothy, my own self, long ago could climb d'plam veree easy." Or hinting, and I guess looking up at them, "Phill-eep, I do believe you b'gettin' outrageous strong 'ere on d'islan'."

He made a point of saying that if he were only fifty again, he could climb the tree and slice them off with his knife. But at seventy-odd, he did not think he could make it to the top.

That morning over breakfast, Timothy said, looking to the tops of the palms, I'm sure, "A lil' milk from d'coconut would b'good now, eh, Phill-eep?"

As yet, I didn't have the courage to climb the palms. "Yes, it would," I said.

Timothy cleared his throat, sighed deeply, and put the coconuts out of his mind. But I knew he'd try me again.

He said, "Dem devilin' coconuts aside, your mutthur would nevei be knowin' you now."

I asked why.

"You are veree brown an' veree lean," he said.

I tried to imagine how I looked. I knew my shirt and pants were in tatters. My hair felt ropy. There was no way to comb it. I wondered how my eyes looked and asked Timothy about that.

"Dey look widout cease," he said. "Dey stare, Phill-eep."

"Do they bother you?"

Timothy laughed. "Not me. Eeevery day I tink what rare good luck I 'ave dat you be 'ere wid my own self on dis outrageous, hombug islan'."

I thought awhile and then asked him, "How long was it before that friend of yours, that friend in the Barbados, could see again?"

Timothy replied vaguely, "Oh, many mont', I do recall."

"But you told me on the raft it was only three days."

"Did I say dat?"

"Yes!"

"Well," Timothy said, "'twas a long time ago. But 'e got 'is sight back, to be true." He paused a moment, then said, "Now, I tell you, we got much wark to do today."

I noticed more and more that Timothy always changed the subject when we began to talk about my eyes. He would make any kind of an excuse.

"What work?" I asked.

"Now, lemme see," he said. "For one ting, we mus' make another catchment . . . an' we mus' go to d'reef for food . . . an' . . ."

I waited.

Timothy finally exploded. "Now, dat is a lot o' wark, Phill-eep, to be true."

Chapter 11

Timothy had fashioned a cane for me, and I was now using it to feel my way around the island. I fell down often, but unless I fell into sea grape, it did not hurt. Even then, I only got a few scratches.

Slowly, I was beginning to know the island. By myself, keeping my feet in the damp sand, which meant I was near the water, I walked the whole way around it. Timothy was very proud of me.

From walking over it, feeling it, and listening to it, I think I knew what our cay looked like. As Timothy said, it was shaped like a melon, or a turtle, sloped up from the sea to our ridge where the palms flapped all day and night in the light trade wind.

The beach, I now believed, was about forty yards wide in most places, stretching all the way around the island. On one end, to the east, was a low coral reef that extended several hundred yards, awash in many places.

I know it was to the east because one morning I was down there with Timothy when the sun came up, and I could feel the warmth on my face from that direction.

The sea grape, a few feet tall at the edge of the beach, and higher farther back, grew along the slopes of the hill on all sides. There was also some other brush that did not feel like sea grape, but Timothy did not know the name of it.

To the south, the beach sloped gradually out into the water. On the north side, it was different. There were submerged coral reefs and great shelves. The water became deep very abruptly. Timothy warned against going into the water here because the sharks could swim close to shore.

Timothy said that the water all around the cay was clear and that he could see many beautiful fish. There was brain coral and organpipe coral that the parrot fish would nibble.

From what I could feel and hear, our cay seemed a lovely island and I wished that I could see it. I planned to walk around it at least once a day, following the vine rope from the ridge to the beach, then setting out along the sand.

I was starting to be less dependent on the vine rope, and sometimes it seemed to me that Timothy was trying hard to make me independent of him. I thought I knew why, but I did not talk to him about it. I did not want to think about the possibility of Timothy dying and leaving me alone on the cay.

Because the rain the night before had made us hopeful, I think both of us did our chores with one ear to the sky, listening for the sound of engines. But all day we heard nothing but familiar sounds, the surf, the wind, and the cries of sea birds.

That night after dinner, Timothy grumbled, "No aircraft! D'islan' mus' 'ave a jumbi."

"Don't talk nonsense, Timothy," I said.

"D'evil spirit harass an' meliss us," he said darkly. "An' we do not 'ave a chicken or grains o' corn to chase 'im."

I said, "Timothy, you can't really believe in that."

My father had told me about "obediah," or "voodoo," in the West Indies. It had come over from Africa, of course. Haiti was the worst of all for it, but there was some practice on all the islands. It was mixed up with religion and witch doctors.

I knew he was looking at Stew Cat when he said, "Mebbe dat outrageous cat is d'jumbi."

"He's just an old cat, Timothy," I protested.

Recalling everything that had happened, Timothy said, "He came board d'raff, an' we got separated from all else; den d'young bahss' eyes got dark, gibbin' us exceedin' trouble; den we float up dis hombuggin' Debil's Mout' . . ."

Angrily, I said, "Timothy, Stew Cat is not a jumbi. You let him alone."

The old man was silent, and I was suddenly worried for Stew Cat's safety. Timothy stayed by me all night but in the morning, when I awakened, he was gone and so was Stew Cat.

I crawled out of the hut and began to call for Stew. Then I called for Timothy. There was no answer. I went down the hill and headed up the beach toward the reef. Voodoo was silly, I knew, but it was also frightening. I couldn't understand why Timothy thought Stew Cat was the jumbi.

I decided to circle the island to find them. Using my cane to feel the way, to touch driftwood or coral ledges the night tide might have uncovered, I moved along the damp sand, calling out now and then.

When I reached the north side, Timothy answered, "Marnin', Phill-eep."

I asked him where he'd been.

He laughed. "Dere is lil' place to go 'ere. I 'ave been 'ere on dis beach."

"Where is Stew Cat?"

Timothy was silent.

I asked again.

"B'gettin' his own self a lizzard, mebbe, mebbe,"

he answered, but there was something conniving in his voice.

All the while, I could hear a scraping noise and, occasionally, a ring of metal. "What are you doing?" I asked.

"Cuttin' on an ol' piece o' wood," he replied.

Why would he be down on north beach this early cutting wood? I knew we had plenty for the campfire and the signal fire.

"And you haven't seen Stew Cat?"

"Not a 'air," he said.

I wanted to see what he had in his hands, but I didn't have the courage to walk up and touch it. I said, "Timothy, I'm very hungry."

I felt his hand on my wrist. He said, "We'll go to d'hut."

He fixed breakfast, we ate, and then without a word, he slipped away.

Usually, he kept his hunting knife in the tin box that had stored our biscuits. Also in that box were the dry matches we had left, a few pieces of stale chocolate, and small things that Timothy had salvaged from the beach or the raft.

I felt a few nails, the hinges that had been on the raft's trap door, some short lengths of rope, a piece of cork, several small tin cans, and a small roll of something that felt like leather. Nothing was missing except the knife, and I knew he'd taken it to north beach with him.

As best I could, I searched around the hut area for Stew Cat, thinking maybe Timothy had tied him up somewhere. Yet I was certain he'd be meowing if he was within hearing distance.

I was positive that Timothy was back on north beach cutting on that piece of wood but something told me not to go down there. So I sat by the hut wondering what to do. It was no good trying to convince him that jumbi did not exist, nor was there any way to find Stew Cat if Timothy had hidden him.

The morning hours passed slowly. Once, I went down to east beach to sit near the signal fire, hoping to hear the drone of an aircraft. Several times, over the stir of the wind, I thought I heard a faint meow, but I couldn't locate the direction.

Maybe all that had happened was beginning to work on the old man's mind. Maybe I was stranded on a tiny, forgotten island in the Caribbean with a madman. If he harmed Stew Cat because of some silly jumbi thing, I knew he might also harm me.

I thought about getting back on the raft and letting it drift to sea again. I was certain that there were enough boards still on top to sit and sleep on. If I could get the water keg down the hill, and the last pieces of chocolate out of the box, I'd be all right for a few days.

I got up and went down to the water, feeling my way toward the reef. I knew that if I kept going that way, I'd touch or fall over the length of life-line rope that tethered the raft. Timothy had driven a heavy piece of driftwood into the sand so that the raft would not go out to sea with the tide.

I walked slowly and carefully, expecting at any moment to feel the rope with my cane, or have it hit against my ankles. I went all the way to the beginning of the reef without finding it. Then I reversed my course, and walked in the other direction. Finally, I stumbled over the heavy piece of wood that Timothy had driven into the sand.

I felt around it, but the rope was no longer tied to it. He'd cut the raft loose! Panic swept over me. But taking my bearing from the stake, I decided to go out into the water, hoping to find the raft.

A few feet offshore, I got another bad scare. I put my foot down and something moved. In fact the whole bottom seemed to move. I lost my balance and fell headfirst into the water. I came up sputtering, and realized I'd stepped on a skate, that diamond-shaped fish with a stinger tail. I'd done that once or twice at Westpunt. The skate is kin to the deadly sea ray, but this one was as shocked as I was and swam off to deep water.

I went out to my waist, feeling with my hands in all directions. But the raft was gone!

I trusted Timothy, and kept telling myself that he wouldn't harm me, but it was the whole mysterious jumbi thing that was frightening. And he certainly wasn't acting like the Timothy I'd been living with.

In midafternoon he returned to the hut. Neither of us spoke.

Then I heard him pounding something. The palm fronds on the hut rattled; whatever it was, he was pounding it into the hut. Having finished, he went away again.

When I heard him moving through the sea grape down the path, I got up and began feeling around the framing of the hut. There was nothing on the sides of it, and I decided that whatever he'd attached had to be on the roof.

I knew there were several lengths of log over near the campfire. So I approached it, found one of the logs, and rolled it over to the entrance to the hut. I stood on it and felt along the crossframe that held the roof up.

In the very center I found what I was looking for. I

cried out when the palm of my hand touched something sharp. Then with my fingers, I slowly felt around the object. It had a head, I discovered, four feet, and a tail.

Timothy had spent all that time carving a cat, a Stew Cat. The nails in it were supposed to kill the evil jumbi.

I felt weak and sat down on the log.

Soon, he came up the path, dropping Stew Cat into my lap.

"Where was he?" I asked.

"On d'raff, o' course," Timothy answered. "I got 'im off d'islan' till I could chase d'jumbi."

"Where is the raft, Timothy?"

"'Twas off d'shore, Phill-eep. 'Tis back now. An' our luck is change."

But it didn't change. It got worse.

Chapter 12

One morning in the middle of May, I awakened to hear Timothy taking great breaths. It sounded as though he were fighting for air. I listened a moment and then asked, "Are you all right, Timothy?"

He wheezed back, "Feber! Malar!"

I had to think a moment to understand what he was talking about. Fever! Malaria! I reached over to touch him. His forehead was burning hot.

His breath coming in big, harsh sighs, he said, "I got malar agin, Phill-eep. 'Twill go away, but fetch some wattah."

When I had had fever in Virginia, and at Scharloo, my mother had given me aspirin and then put cold cloths on my head. But we had no aspirin on the cay, of course, and the water was always warm. I poured some water from the keg, and gave it to him. He gulped it and then fell back on the mat.

For a while, I listened to his heavy breathing and then ripped a piece of cloth from what was left of my shirt, dampened it with water, and placed it on his forehead. He murmured, "Dat be good," but suddenly he began to shiver, even though the morning air was already warm. I could hear his teeth clacking.

I had nothing to cover him with, so I just sat beside him holding the cloth, which was already beginning to dry, to his forehead. His breath was like air from a furnace.

It must have been about ten o'clock when Timothy began to mumble and laugh. It sounded almost as if he were talking in his sleep, but the laughter, little bursts of it between the wheezes, was very high and strange. I couldn't keep the cloth on his head because he was tossing from side to side.

I talked to him constantly, but he didn't even seem to know I was there.

Once he got up but fell back down to the mat, and I told him to stay very still. For a long time, he did, because he began to shiver again. When that ended, the mumbling and high laughter started all over.

At about noontime, the mumbling got worse, and I could feel him trying to get to his feet. I clung to his arm, shouting for him to lie down again, but he threw me aside as if I weren't there. I could hear him crashing down the hill toward the sea, the frightening laughter echoing back.

I followed the trail of laughter. Then I heard splashing and knew he'd gone into the water. I yelled, "Timothy, Timothy, come back."

Suddenly it became dead quiet. I screamed his name again and again. There was no answer.

I reached the beach and waded out to my knees, then began to move slowly along, trying to keep on a line with the beach. I had gone about thirty steps when I fell over Timothy's body, plunging down in the water.

Holding onto him with one hand, I got on my feet again. The upper part of his body was floating but I knew his feet were dragging on the bottom. I put my face against his mouth. Yes, he was still breathing.

I worked myself around to put both hands under his shoulders, but he was too heavy that way. Then I clasped my hands under his chin, and began to pull him out. He made strange sounds, but did not try to help me.

It took me what seemed like a long time to get Timothy out of the water and back up on the damp sand. He must have weighed two hundred and twenty or thirty pounds, and I could only move him two or three inches at a time.

I sat beside him for almost an hour in the hot sun while he rested quietly, his breathing not so harsh now. Then I realized he was shivering again. I knew I could not drag him up the slope to the shelter of the hut, so I tore off branches of sea grape and put them over his body. The grape leaves cut the rays of the sun.

I brought water down from the hut, raised his head, and ordered him to drink it. With one hand, I found his lips and then guided the cup to his chin. He seemed to understand and gulped it down.

I stayed by him the rest of the long afternoon while he slept. When he awakened, it was early evening and had turned cool again. He was breathing easily now, and I knew the fever had broken because his forehead was no longer hot.

Sitting up, he said weakly, "How did I get downg 'ere?"

I told him he'd run down the hill.

"Dat debil, d'fever," Timothy sighed.

I said, "You went into the water. You scared me, Timothy."

"Dat be true," he said. "My 'ead burn wid fire, an' I put it out."

I helped him to his feet, and we went up the hill together, Timothy leaning on me for support for the first time. He never really regained his strength.

Chapter **13**

It was in late May that I believe Timothy decided we might stay there forever. We had not seen a schooner sail or heard an airplane since setting foot on the island.

I knew it was late May because each day he dropped a small pebble into an old can that he'd found on the beach. It was our only way to tell how many days we'd been there. Every so often, I'd count them, beginning with April 9. We now had forty-eight pebbles in the can.

On this day, Timothy said thoughtfully, "Phill-eep, 'as it evah come into your own self that I might be poorly again some marnin'?" I knew he was thinking about malar and the fever.

I said it had.

He said, "Well, you mus' den know how to provite your own self wid feesh."

For more than a week, I knew he had been laboring over nails to turn them into fish hooks. He always speared the fish or langosta with a sharp stick, but I could not see, of course, to do that. I knew he was making the hooks for me.

He said, with a secret tone in his voice, "I 'ave foun' an outrageous good 'ole on d'reef in a safe place."

We went down the hill and started out along the reef shelf. By now, my feet were tough and I hardly felt the jagged edges of the coral. But I knew that lurking in the tide pools were the treacherous sea urchins. Stepping on them invited a sharp spine in your foot, and Timothy had already warned me that, "dey veree poison, dey b'gibbin' you terrible pain."

Every two feet, Timothy had driven a piece of driftwood deep into the coral crevices so that I could feel them as I went along. Neither of us knew what to do about the sea urchins but Timothy said he'd think mightily about them. He had taken a large rock to smash them all along the path over the reef top. But in time they would come back.

We went out about fifty feet along the reef, and then he said, "Now, we feesh."

He described the hole to me. It was about twenty feet in diameter and six to eight feet deep. The bottom was sandy, but mostly free of coral so that my hooks would not snag. He said there was a "mos'" natural opening to the sea, so that the fish could swim in and out of this coral-walled pool.

He took my hand to have me feel all around the edges of the hole. The coral had been smoothed over by centuries of sea wash. Timothy said that the sand in the sea water acted like a grindstone on the sharp edges of the coral. It was not completely smooth but there were no jagged edges sticking out.

"Now, reach downg 'ere," Timothy said, "an' tug off d'mussel."

I put my hand into the warm water, kneeling down over the ledge, and felt a mussel. But in ripping it loose, I lost my balance and only Timothy's hand prevented me from falling in. If you are blind, the sensation of falling can be terrifying. My memory of the fall off the raft was still very clear.

Timothy said, "Easy dere, Phill-eep. Jus' sit a moment an' relax."

His voice was soothing. "If evah you do fall, jus'

stay in d'hole awhile, feel which way d'wattah washes, den follow it to d'ledge, grab hol', an' pull your own self out."

Timothy guided my hands in opening the tough mussel shell and digging the slippery meat out to bait the hook. "'Tis an outrageous sharp knife, so be veree careful o' your fingers."

Then he told me to feel the hook and slip the mussel bait over the barb. I'd fished many times with my father and this was easy.

Rusty bolts served as sinkers. Timothy had found several pieces of wood with bolts in them; had burned them, then raked the bolts out of the ashes. He'd unraveled a life line from the raft to make single strands for the fishing line.

I dropped the hook and sinker overboard. In a moment, there was a sharp tug. I jerked, flipping the fish back over my shoulder so it would land on the reef. Timothy cheered and told me to feel along the line to the wriggling fish, then take the hook out.

Squirming and jumping in my hand, it was small but fat. I grinned over toward Timothy. When I had fished before, it was fun. Now, I felt I had done something very special. I was learning to do things all over again, by touch and feel.

I said to Timothy, "Dis is outrageous, hom-buggin' good feesh 'ole."

He laughed with pleasure.

Every day after that I did all the fishing. Timothy, of course, continued to get langosta. He had to dive for them, but I caught all the fish. After the third morning, he let me go out alone on the reef. I'd feel my way along his driftwood stobs, find the hole, pry a mussel loose, and then fish.

I was alone on the reef but somehow I always felt

he was sitting on the beach nearby. I could sense his presence, yet he was always at the hut when I got back there.

We often talked about the cay and what was on it. Timothy had not thought much about it. He took it for granted that the cay was always there, but I told him about geography, and how maybe a volcano could have caused the Devil's Mouth. He'd listen in fascination, almost speechless.

We talked about how the little coral animals might have been building the foundations of the cay for thousands of years. I said, "Then sand began to gather on it, and after more years, it was finally an island."

It was as if a new world had opened up for Timothy. He kept using that same expression, "Dat be true?"

I found out that he'd never thought about how the sea grape, or the vines, or the coconuts came to our cay. I told him what I knew.

Seeds had drifted in from the sea, or birds had brought them. After a rain, they'd taken root.

"D'lizzard?" he asked sternly.

"I'd bet a bird, flying from another island, holding a mother lizard in its beak, dropped it here. Then the baby lizards were born. Or maybe a mother lizard washed ashore on driftwood during a storm."

Timothy was very impressed, and I felt good that I'd been able to tell him something.

We found a lot to talk about.

I think it was the fifth afternoon of this week that I blurted out to Timothy, "I'll climb the palm now."

"Eh, Phill-eep," he said, and I could almost see the grin on his face and the light in his eyes as he looked skyward. Greedily, I'm sure.

He said, "Dere is one coconut tree ovah dere dat 'as a sway in 'is back like an ol' horse. Dat is d'one to clim'."

I was trembling a little as he led me to the tree, telling me I should go up just a short way; climb it like a monkey. If I could do it, I was to come back down, put the knife between my teeth, and go up again.

The trunk of this palm tree must have been about two feet in diameter because I could easily put my hands around to the back. I grasped it, hunched my body, placed my bare feet on the rough trunk, and began to climb. Timothy was probably holding his breath.

I went up about ten feet and froze. I could not move up or down. My legs and arms were rigid.

Timothy, standing below to catch me if I fell, called up softly, "Phill-eep, 'tis no shame to ease your own self back downg to d'san'."

Slowly I began to back down along the trunk. The bark was rough against my hands and feet, but what I felt most was Timothy's disappointment. I couldn't have been more than a few feet off the ground when I took a deep breath and said to myself, If you fall, you'll fall in sand.

Then I started climbing again.

Timothy called up, "You 'ave forgot d'knife."

I knew that if I stopped now, I'd never climb it. I didn't answer him but kept my hands and feet moving steadily. Then I heard him shout, "You b'gettin' to d'top." Palm fronds brushed my head. I grasped the base of one to pull myself up. Timothy let out a roar of joy.

Then he told me how to reach the coconuts. It took a long time to pull, tug, and twist two of them loose.

But they finally fell. I stayed in the palm another few minutes to rest, then slid down. I had won.

As my feet touched the ground, Timothy hugged me, yelling, "D'palm harass us no more."

We drank every drop of the coconut milk, and feasted on the fresh meat.

Squatting near me, his teeth crunching the coconut, Timothy said, "You see, Phill-eep, you do not need d'eye now. You 'ave done widout d'eye what I couldn't do wid my whole body."

It was almost as if I'd graduated from the survival course that Timothy had been putting me through since we had landed on the cay.

It rained that night, a very soft rain. Not even enough to drip through the palm frond roof. Timothy breathed softly beside me. I had now been with him every moment of the day and night for two months, but I had not seen him. I remembered that ugly welted face. But now, in my memory, it did not seem ugly at all. It seemed only kind and strong.

I asked, "Timothy, are you still black?"

His laughter filled the hut.

Chapter 14

One very hot morning in July, we were down on north beach where Timothy had found a patch of calico scallops not too far offshore. It was the hottest day we'd ever had on the cay. So hot that each breath felt like fire. And for once, the trade wind was not blowing. Nothing on the cay seemed to be moving.

North beach was a very strange beach anyway. The sand on it felt coarser to my feet. Everything about it felt different, but that didn't really make sense since it was only about a mile from south beach.

Timothy explained, "D'nawth is alles d'bleak beach on any islan'," but he couldn't say why.

He had just brought some calico scallops ashore when we heard the rifle shot. He came quickly to my side, saying, "Dat b'trouble."

Trouble? I thought it meant someone had found the cay. That wasn't trouble. Excited, I asked, "Who's shooting?"

"D'sea," he said.

I laughed at him, "The sea can't shoot a rifle."

"A crack like d'rifle," he said, worry in his voice. "It can make d'shot all right, all right. It b'tell us a veree bad starm is comin', Phill-eep. A tempis'."

I couldn't quite believe that. However, there had been, distinctly, a crack like a rifle or pistol shot.

He said anxiously, "D'waves do it. Somewhar far off, out beyond d'Grenadines, or in dat pesky bight off Honduras, a hurrican' is spawnin', young bahss. I feel it. What we heeard was a wave passin' dis lil' hombug point."

I heard him sniffing the air as if he could smell the hurricane coming. Without the wind, there was a breathless silence around our cay. The sea, he told me, was smooth as green jelly. But already, the water was getting cloudy. There were no birds in sight. The sky, he said, had a yellowish cast to it.

"Come along, we 'ave much to do. D'calico scallop can wait dey own self till after d'tempis'."

We went up to our hill.

Now I knew why he had chosen the highest point of land on the cay for our hut. Even so, I thought, the waves might tumble over it.

The first thing Timothy did was to lash our water keg high on a palm trunk. Next he took the remaining rope that we had and tied it securely around the same sturdy tree. "In case d'tempis' reach dis high, lock your arms ovah d'rope an' hang on, Phill-eep."

I realized then why he had used our rope sparingly; why he had made my guideline down to east beach from vines instead of rope. Everyday, I learned of something new that Timothy had done so we could survive.

During the afternoon, he told me this was a freak storm, because most did not come until September or October. August, sometimes. Seldom in July. "But dis year, d'sea be angry wid all d'death upon it. D'wahr."

The storms bred, Timothy said, in the eastern North Atlantic, south of the Cape Verde Islands, in the fall, but sometimes, when they were freaks, and early, they bred much closer, in a triangle way off the northeast tip of South America. Once in a great while, in June or July, they sometimes made up not far from Providencia and San Andrés. Near us. The June ones were only pesky, but the July ones were dangerous.

"Dis be a western starm, I b'guessin'. Dey outrageous strong when dey come," he said.

Even Stew Cat was nervous. He was around my legs whenever I moved. I asked Timothy what we should do to protect him. He laughed. "Stew Cat b'go up d'palm on d'lee side iffen it b'gettin' too terrible. Don' worry 'bout Stew Cat."

Yet I could not help worrying. The thought of losing either of them was unbearable. If something had happened on the cay, I wanted it to happen to all of us.

Nothing changed during the afternoon, although it seemed to get even hotter. Timothy spent a lot of time down at the raft, stripping off everything usable and carrying it back up the hill. He said we might never see it again, or else it might wash up the hill so that it would be impossible to launch.

Timothy was not purposely trying to frighten me about the violence of the storm; he was just being honest. He had good reason to be frightened himself.

"In '28, I be on d'*Hettie Redd* sout' o' Antigua when d'tempis' hit. D'wind was outrageous, an' d'ol' schooner break up like chips fallin' 'fore d'ax. I wash ashore from d'sea, so wild no mahn believe it. No odder mahn from d'*Hettie Redd* live 'ceptin' me."

I knew that wild sea from long ago was much on Timothy's mind all afternoon.

We had a huge meal late in the day, much bigger than usual, because Timothy said we might not be able to eat for several days. We had fish and coconut meat, and we each drank several cups of coconut milk. Timothy said that the fish might not return to the reef for at least a week. He'd noticed that they'd already gone to deep water.

After we ate, Timothy carefully cleaned his knife and put it into the tin box, which he lashed high on the same tree that held our water keg.

"We ready, Phill-eep," he said.

Chapter 15

At sunset, with the air heavy and hot, Timothy described the sky to me. He said it was flaming red and that there were thin veils of high clouds. It was so still over our cay that we could hear nothing but the rustling of the lizards.

Just before dark, Timothy said, "'Twon't be long now, Phill-eep."

We felt a light breeze that began to ripple the smooth sea. Timothy said he saw an arc of very black clouds to the west. They looked as though they were beginning to join the higher clouds.

I gathered Stew Cat close to me as we waited, feeling the warm breeze against my face. Now and then, there were gusts of wind that rattled the palm fronds, shaking the little hut.

It was well after dark when the first drops of rain spattered the hut, and with them, the wind turned cool. When it gusted, the rain hit the hut like handfuls of gravel.

Then the wind began to blow steadily, and Timothy went out of the hut to look up at the sky. He shouted, "Dey boilin' ovah now, Phill-eep. 'Tis hurrican', to be sure."

We could hear the surf beginning to crash as the wind drove waves before it, and Timothy ducked back inside to stand in the opening of the hut, his big body stretched so that he could hang onto the overhead frame, keeping the hut erect as long as possible.

I felt movement around my legs and feet. Things were slithering. I screamed to Timothy who shouted back, "B'nothin' but d'lil' lizzard, comin' high groun'."

Rain was now slashing into the hut, and the wind was reaching a steady howl. The crash of the surf sounded closer; I wondered if it was already beginning to push up toward our hill. The rain was icy, and I was wet, head to foot. I was shivering, but more from the thought of the sea rolling over us than from the sudden cold.

In a moment, there was a splintering sound, and Timothy dropped down beside me, covering my body with his. Our hut had blown away. He shouted, "Phill-eep, put your 'ead downg." I rolled over on my stomach, my cheek against the wet sand. Stew Cat burrowed down between us.

There was no sound now except the roar of the storm. Even the sound of the wind was being beaten down by the wildness of the sea. The rain was hitting my back like thousands of hard berries blown from air guns.

Once something solid hit us and then rolled on. "Sea grape," Timothy shouted. It was being torn up by the roots.

We stayed flat on the ground for almost two hours, taking the storm's punishment, barely able to breathe in the driving rain. Then Timothy shouted hoarsely, "To d'palm."

The sea was beginning to reach for our hilltop, climbing the forty feet with raging whitecaps. Timothy dragged me toward the palm. I held Stew Cat against my chest.

Standing with his back to the storm, Timothy put

my arms through the loops of rope, and then roped himself, behind me, to the tree.

Soon, I felt water around my ankles. Then it washed to my knees. It would go back and then crash against us again. Timothy was taking the full blows of the storm, sheltering me with his body. When the water receded, it would tug at us, and Timothy's strength would fight against it. I could feel the steel in his arms as the water tried to suck us away.

Even in front of him, crushed against the trunk of the palm, I could feel the rain, which was now jabbing into me like the punches of a nail. It was not falling toward earth but being driven straight ahead by the wind.

We must have been against the palm for almost an hour when suddenly the wind died down and the rain became gentle. Timothy panted, "D'eye! We can relax a bit till d'odder side o' d'tempis' hit us."

I remembered that hurricanes, which are great circling storms, have a calm eye in the center.

"Are you all right?" I asked.

He replied hoarsely, "I b'damp, but all right."

Yet I heard him making small noises, as if it were painful to move, as we stood back from the palm trunk. We sat down on the ground beside it, still being pelted with rain, to wait for the eye to pass. Water several inches deep swirled around us, but was not tugging at us.

It was strange and eerie in the eye of the hurricane. I knew we were surrounded on all sides by violent winds, but the little cay was calm and quiet. I reached over for Timothy. He was cradling his head in his arms, still making those small noises, like a hurt animal.

In twenty or thirty minutes, the wind picked up sharply and Timothy said that we must stand against the palm again. Almost within seconds, the full fury of the storm hit the cay once more. Timothy pressed me tightly against the rough bark.

It was even worse this time, but I do not remember everything that happened. We had been there awhile when a wave that must have reached half-way up the palms crashed against us. The water went way over my head. I choked and struggled. Then another giant wave struck us. I lost consciousness then. Timothy did, too, I think.

When I came to, the wind had died down, coming at us only in gusts. The water was still washing around our ankles, but seemed to be going back into the sea now. Timothy was still behind me, but he felt cold and limp. He was sagging, his head down on my shoulder.

"Timothy, wake up," I said.

He did not answer.

Using my shoulders, I tried to shake him, but the massive body did not move. I stood very still to see if he was breathing. I could feel his stomach moving and I reached over my shoulder to his mouth. There was air coming out. I knew that he was not dead.

However, Stew Cat was gone.

I worked for a few minutes to release my arms from the loops of rope around the palm trunk, and then slid out from under Timothy's body. He slumped lifelessly against the palm. I felt along the ropes that bound his forearms to the trunk until I found the knots.

With his weight against them, it was hard to pull them loose, even though they were sailor's knots and had loops in them. The rope was soaked, which made it worse.

I must have worked for half an hour before I had him free from the trunk. He fell backwards into the wet sand, and lay there moaning. I knew there was very little I could do for him except to sit by him in the light rain, holding his hand. In my world of darkness, I had learned that holding a hand could be like medicine.

After a long while, he seemed to recover. His first words, painful and dragged out, were, "Phill-eep . . . you . . . all right . . . be true?"

"I'm okay, Timothy," I said.

He said weakly, "Terrible tempis'."

He must have rolled over on his stomach in the sand, because his hand left mine abruptly. Then he went to sleep, I guess.

I touched his back. It felt warm and sticky. I ran my hand lightly down it, suddenly realizing that I, too, was completely naked. The wind and sea had torn our tatters of clothes from us.

Timothy had been cut to ribbons by the wind, which drove the rain and tiny grains of sand before it. It had flayed his back and his legs until there were very few places that weren't cut. He was bleeding, but there was nothing I could do to stop it. I found his hard, horny hand again, wrapped mine around it, and lay down beside him.

I went to sleep too.

Sometime long after dawn, I awakened. The rain had stopped, and the wind had died down to its usual whisper. But I think the clouds were still covering the sky because I could not feel the sun.

I said, "Timothy," but he did not answer me. His hand was cold and stiff in mine.

Old Timothy, of Charlotte Amalie, was dead.

I stayed there beside him for a long time, very

tired, thinking that he should have taken me with him wherever he had gone. I did not cry then. There are times when you are beyond tears.

I went back to sleep, and this time when I awakened, I heard a meow. Then I cried for a long time, holding Stew Cat tight. Aside from him, I was blind and alone on a forgotten cay.

Chapter 16

In the afternoon, I groped west along the hill. Thirty or forty feet from the last palm tree, I began to dig a grave for Timothy. I cleared palm fronds, chunks of sea grape, pieces of wood, dead fish, fan coral, and shells that the sea had thrown up. I marked out a space about seven feet long and four feet wide. Then I dug with my hands.

At first I was angry with Timothy. I said to Stew Cat, "Why did he leave us alone here?" Then as I dug, I had other thoughts.

With his great back to the storm, taking its full punishment, he had made it possible for me to live. When my grandfather died, my father had said, "Phillip, sometimes people die from just being very, very tired." I think that is what happened to Timothy.

I also think that had I been able to see, I might not have been able to accept it all. But strangely, the darkness separated me from everything. It was as if my blindness were protecting me from fear.

I buried Timothy, placing stones at the head of the grave to mark it. I didn't know what to say over the grave. I said. "Thank you, Timothy," and then turned my face to the sky. I said, "Take care of him, God, he was good to me."

There didn't seem to be anything else to say, so I just stood by his grave for a while. Then I felt my way back to the spot where our hut had been. I located wood and piled it around the base of the palm tree that held our water keg and the tin box. Both were to the lee side of the storm.

It took me a long time to get the keg and the tin box to the ground, but I found, on opening the bung, that the water was still sweet and that the matches, wrapped in cellophane inside the tin box, were dry. But the two small bars of chocolate that we had been saving for a "feast," were ruined. I had no taste for them, anyway.

Feeling it everywhere under my feet, I knew that the cay was littered with debris. I started cleaning the camp area, or what was left of it. I piled all the palm fronds, frayed by the wind, in one place; sticks of wet driftwood in another.

With Stew Cat constantly around—I stumbled over him several times—I worked until I felt it was nearing darkness. I'd found one lone coconut in a mass of sea grape and broken sticks. I opened it and ate the meat, offering to share with Stew Cat, who didn't seem interested.

Then I made a bed of palm fronds and sprawled out on it, listening to the still angry sea as it tumbled around the damp cay and thinking: I must feed myself and Stew Cat; I must rebuild the hut and build another signal fire down on east beach; then I must spend each day listening for the sound of aircraft. I knew Timothy had already given up on any schooner entering the dangerous Devil's Mouth.

I was certain that the sea had washed away Timothy's markers atop the coral reef, and I was also sure that my guide vine-rope leading down to the beach had been snapped and tangled by the storm.

But now, for the first time, I fully understood why Timothy had so carefully trained me to move around the island, and the reef . . .

The reef, I thought.

How could I fish without any poles? They must have been washed away. Then I remembered Timothy saying that he would put them in a safe place. The trouble was he'd forgotten to tell me where.

I got up and began to run my hands over each palm trunk. On one of them I touched rope. I followed it around to the lee side with my fingers. And there they were! Not two or three, but at least a dozen, lashed together, each with a barbed hook and bolt sinker. They were one more part of the legacy Timothy had left me.

The sun came out strong in the morning. I could feel it on my face. It began to dry the island, and toward noon, I heard the first cry of a bird. They were returning.

By now, I had taught myself to tell time, very roughly, simply by turning my head toward the direct warmth of the sun. If the angle was almost overhead, I knew it was around noon. If it was low, then of course, it was early morning or late evening.

There was so much to do that I hardly knew where to start. Get a campfire going, pile new wood for a signal fire, make another rain catchment for the water keg, weave a mat of palm fibers to sleep on. Then make a shelter of some kind, fish the hole on the reef, inspect the palm trees to see if any coconuts were left—I didn't think any could be up there—and search the whole island to discover what the storm had deposited. It was enough work for weeks, and I said to Stew Cat, "I don't know how we'll get it all done." But something told me I must stay very busy and not think about myself.

I accomplished a lot in three days, even putting a

new edge on Timothy's knife by honing it on coral. I jabbed it into the palm nearest my new shelter, so that I would always know where it was if I needed it. Without Timothy's eyes, I was finding that in my world, everything had to be very precise; an exact place for everything.

On the fifth day after the storm, I began to scour the island to find out what had been cast up. It was exciting, and I knew it would take days or weeks to accomplish. I had made another cane, and beginning with east beach, I felt my way back and forth, reaching down to touch everything that my cane struck; sometimes having to spend a long time trying to decide what it was that I held in my hands.

I found several large cans and used one of them to start the "time" can again, dropping five pebbles into it so that the reckoning would begin again from the night of the storm. I discovered an old broom, and a small wooden crate that would make a nice stool. I found a piece of canvas and tried to think of ways to make pants from it, but I had no needle or thread.

Other than that, I found many shells, some bodies of dead birds, pieces of cork, and chunks of sponge, but nothing I could really put to good use.

It was on the sixth day after the storm, when I was exploring on south beach, that I heard the birds. Stew Cat was with me, as usual, and he growled when they first screeched. Their cries were angry, and I guessed that seven or eight might be in the air.

I stood listening to them; wondering what they were. Then I felt a beat of wing past my face, and an angry cry as the bird dived at me. I lashed out at it with my cane, wondering why they were attacking me.

Another dived down, screaming at me, and his bill nipped the side of my head. For a moment, I was confused, not knowing whether to run for cover under sea grape, or what was left of it, or try to fight them off with my cane. There seemed to be a lot of birds.

Then one pecked my forehead sharply, near my eyes, and I felt blood run down my face. I started to walk back toward camp, but had taken no more than three or four steps when I tripped over a log. I fell into the sand, and at the same time, felt a sharp pain in the back of my head. I heard a raging screech as the bird soared up again. Then another bird dived at me.

I heard Stew Cat snarling and felt him leap up on my back, his claws digging into my flesh. There was another wild screech, and Stew Cat left my back, leaping into the air.

His snarls and the wounded screams of the bird filled the stillness over the cay. I could hear them battling in the sand. Then I heard the death caw of the bird.

I lay still a moment. Finally, I crawled to where Stew Cat had his victim. I touched him; his body was rigid and his hair was still on edge. He was growling, low and muted.

Then I touched the bird. It had sounded large, but it was actually rather small. I felt the beak; it was very sharp.

Slowly, Stew Cat began to relax.

Wondering what had caused the birds to attack me, I felt around in the sand. Soon, my hand touched a warm shell. I couldn't blame the birds very much. I'd accidentally walked into their new nesting ground.

They were fighting for survival, after the storm, just as I was. I left Stew Cat to his unexpected meal and made my way slowly back to camp.

Chapter 17

Ten pebbles had gone into my "time" can when I decided to do something Timothy had told me never to do. I was tired of eating fish and sea-grape leaves, and I wanted to save the few green coconuts I'd managed to find on the ground. There were none left in the trees.

I wanted scallops or a langosta to roast over the fire. I didn't dare go out off north beach for scallops because of the sharks. But I thought there might be a langosta clinging to coral at the bottom of the fishing hole.

From what Timothy had told me, the sea entrance to the hole was too narrow for a large fish, a shark, to swim through. Barracuda, he'd said, could go through, but they were not usually dangerous. If there happened to be an octopus down there, it would have to be a very small one. The big ones were always in deep water. So he'd said it was safe for him to dive in the hole.

I sharpened a stick the way Timothy had done, but I knew that if I felt a langosta with my left hand, I would have to be very quick with my right hand, or he would use his tail to push away from me across the sand.

With Stew Cat, I went down to the reef and felt my way along it until I found the familiar edges of the hole. I told Stew Cat, "If I'm not out in twenty minutes, you better jump in and get me."

The crazy cat rubbed along my leg and purred.

Holding the sharpened stick in my right hand, I slipped into the warm water, treading for a moment, waiting to see if anything came up. Then I ducked my head underwater, swam down a few feet, and came up again. I was certain that nothing was in the hole aside from the usual small fish I yanked out each morning.

After a few minutes, I had my courage up and dived to the bottom, holding the sharp stick in my left hand now, and using my right hand to feel the coral and rocks. Coming up now and then for air, I slowly felt my way around the bottom of the small pool, touching sea fans that waved back and forth, feeling the organpipe coral and the bigger chunks of brain coral.

Several times I was startled when seaweed or sea fans would brush against my face and swam quickly to the surface. It must have taken me nearly thirty minutes to decide that I could hunt langosta in the hole.

This time, I dived in earnest. I went straight down, touched the bottom, and then took a few strokes toward the coral sides of the pool. Timothy had said that langosta were always on the bottom, usually over against the rocks and coral. To my amazement, I touched one on the first sweep and drove the sharp stick into him, swimming quickly to the surface.

Panting, I shouted to Stew Cat, "Lobster tonight!"

I swam to the edge, pushed the langosta off the stick, caught my breath again, and dived.

I dived many times without again touching the hard shell that meant langosta. I began sticking my hands deeper into the shelves and over the ledges near the bottom.

I rested a few minutes, then decided I'd make one

more dive. I was happy with the lobster that was now on the reef, but it was quite small, barely a meal for Stew Cat and myself.

I dived again, and this time found what seemed to be an opening into a deep hole. Or at least, the hole went far back. There has to be a big lobster in there, I thought. Up I came again, filled my lungs, and dived immediately.

I ran my hand back into the hole, and something grabbed it.

Terrified, I put my feet against the rocks to pull away. The pain was severe. Whatever had my wrist had the strength of Timothy's arms. I jerked hard and whatever it was came out with my arm, its tail smashing against my chest. I kicked and rose to the surface, the thing still on my wrist, its teeth sunk in deep.

I'm sure I screamed as I broke water, flailing toward the edge of the hole. Then the thing let loose, and I made it up over the side and out of the hole.

Pain shooting up my entire arm, I lay panting on the edge of the pool and gingerly began to feel my wrist. It was bleeding, but not badly. But the teeth had sunk in deep.

It wasn't a fish, because the body felt long and narrow. Some time later, I made an informed guess that it had been a large moray eel. Whatever it was, I never got back into the hole again.

Chapter 18

There was no day or night that passed when I didn't listen for sounds from the sky. Both my sense of touch and my sense of hearing were beginning to make up for my lack of sight. I separated the sounds and each became different.

I grew to know the different cries of the birds that flew by the cay, even though I had no idea what any of them were. I made up my own names for them according to the sound of their cries. Only the occasional bleat of the gull gave me a picture of that bird, for I had heard and seen them many times around the sea wall in Willemstad.

I knew how the breeze sounded when it crossed the sea grape. It fluttered the small leaves. When it went through the palm fronds the storm hadn't ripped away, it made a flapping noise.

I knew the rustle of the lizards. Some were still on the island after the storm. I could only guess they'd somehow climbed high into the palms. Otherwise, how could they have lived with water lapping over the entire cay?

I even knew when Stew Cat was approaching me. His soft paws on a dried leaf made only a tiny crackle, but I heard it.

One midmorning in early August, I was on the hill, near the camp, when I heard the far-off drone of an airplane. It was up-wind from me, but the sound was very clear. I reached down to feel Stew Cat. He had heard it too. His body was tense; his head pointed toward the sound.

I dropped to my knees by the fire, feeling around the edges until I grasped the end of a stick. I drew it back. Timothy had taught me to lay the fire sticks like a wheel, so that the fire burned slowly in the center, but always had a few unburned ends on the outside. I tended the fire a half dozen times each day.

I spit on the stick until I heard a sizzle. Then I knew there was enough fire or charring on it to light off the base of dried palm fronds beneath the signal fire.

I listened again for the drone. Yes, it was still there. Closer now.

I ran down the hill straight to the signal fire, felt around the palm fronds, and then pushed the stick over them. I blew on it until I heard the crackle of flames. In a few minutes the signal fire was roaring, and I ran to south beach where I would be able to hear the aircraft without hearing the crackling fire.

Standing on south beach, I listened. The plane *was* coming closer!

I yelled toward the sky, "Here! Down here!"

I decided to run back to east beach to stand near the fire and the new arrangement of rocks that spelled out "Help."

Thinking any moment the plane would dive and I would hear the roar of its engines across the cay at low altitude, I stood with Stew Cat a few feet from the sloshing surf. I waited and waited, but there was no thundering sound from the sky. I could hear nothing but the crackling of the fire, the washing sound of the surf.

I ran back to south beach, where I stood very still and listened.

The plane had gone!

Slowly, I returned to east beach and sat down in sea-grape shade. I put my head down on my arms and sobbed, feeling no shame for what I was doing.

There seemed to be no hope of ever leaving the cay, yet I knew I could not always live this way. One day I would become ill or another storm would rage against the island. I could never survive alone.

There had been many bad and lonely days and nights, but none as bad as this.

Stew Cat came up, purring, rubbing along my legs. I held him a long time, wondering why the aircraft had not come down when the pilots saw the smoke.

At last I thought, perhaps they didn't see the smoke. I knew it was going up into the sky, but was it white smoke that might be lost in the blue-white sky, or was it dark and oily smoke that would make a smudge against the blueness? There was no way to tell.

If only there were some oily boards! The kind that drifted around the waters of the Schottegat. But I knew that the wood floating up on the beach consisted mostly of branches or stumps that had been in the water for weeks or months. There was nothing in them to make dark smoke.

I began to think of all the things on the island. Green palm fronds might send off dark smoke, but until they were dried, they were too tough to tear off the trees. The vines on north beach might make dark smoke, but the leaves on them were very small.

The sea grape! I snapped some off, feeling it between my fingers. Yes, there was oil in it. I got up and went over to the fire, tossing a piece in. In a moment, I heard it popping the way hot grease pops when it is dropped into water.

I knew how to do it now.

The smoke would rise from the cay in a fat, black column to lead the planes up the Devil's Mouth. If I heard another aircraft, I'd start a fire and then throw bundles of sea grape into it until I was certain a strong signal was going up from the island.

Timothy hadn't thought about black smoke, I was sure. That was it!

Feeling better now, I walked back up the hill to gather the few palm fronds that were left for a new fire base.

I woke up at dawn on the morning of August 20, 1942, to hear thunder and wondered when the first drops of rain would spatter on the roof of the shelter. I heard Stew Cat, down near my feet, let off a low growl.

I said, "It's only thunder, Stew Cat. We need the water."

But as I continued to listen, it did not seem to be thunder. It was a heavy sound, hard and sharp, not rolling. More like an explosion or a series of explosions. It felt as if the cay were shaking. I got up from the mat, moving out from under the shelter.

The air did not feel like rain. It was dry and there was no heavy heat.

"They're explosions, Stew," I said. "Very near us."

Maybe destroyers, I thought. I could not hear any aircraft engines. Maybe destroyers fighting it out with enemy submarines. And those heavy, hard, sharp sounds could be the depth charges that my father said were used by the Navy to sink U-boats.

This time, I didn't bother to take a piece of firewood down to east beach. I dug into the tin box for the cellophane wrapped package of big wooden matches. Four were left. I ran down the hill.

At the signal fire, I searched around for a rock. Finding one, I knelt down by the fire and struck a match against it. Nothing happened. I felt the head of the match. The sulphur had rubbed off. I struck another. It made a small popping noise and then went out.

I had two more matches left, and for a moment, I didn't know whether to use them or run back up the hill to the campfire.

I stopped to listen, feeling sweat trickle down my face. The explosions were still thundering across the sea.

Then I heard the drone of an aircraft. I took a deep breath and struck the next to last match. I heard it flare and ran my left hand over the top of it. There was heat. It was burning.

I reached deep into the fire pile, holding the match there until it began to burn the tips of my fingers. The fire caught and in a moment was roaring.

I ran across the beach to begin pulling sea grape down. I carried the first bundle to the fire and threw it in. Soon, I could smell it burning. It began to pop and crackle as the flames got to the natural oils in the branches.

By the time I had carried ten or fifteen bundles of sea grape to the fire, tumbling them in, I was sure that a column of black smoke was rising into the sky over the cay.

Suddenly, a deafening roar swept overhead. I knew it was an aircraft crossing the cay not much higher than the palms. I could feel the wind from it.

Forgetting for a moment, I yelled, "Timothy, they've come."

The aircraft seemed to be making a sharp turn. It

roared across the cay again, seeming even lower this time because the rush of wind from it was hot. I could smell exhaust fumes.

I yelled, "Down here, down here," and waved my arms.

The plane made another tight circle, coming back almost directly over me. Its engine was screaming.

I shouted at Stew Cat, "We'll be rescued!" But I think that he'd gone to hide in the sea grape.

This time, however, the aircraft did not circle back. It did not make another low pass over the island. I heard the sound going away. Soon, it had vanished completely. Then I realized that the explosions had stopped too.

A familiar silence settled over the cay.

All the strength went out of my body. It was the first real chance of rescue, and maybe there would not be another. The pilot had flown away, perhaps thinking I was just another native fisherman waving at an aircraft. I knew that the color of my skin was very dark now.

Worse, I knew that the smoke might have blotted out the lines of rocks that spelled help.

Feeling very ill, I climbed the slope again, throwing myself down on the mat in the hut. I didn't cry. There was no use in doing that.

I wanted to die.

After a while, I looked over toward Timothy's grave. I said, "Why didn't you take us with you?"

Chapter 19

It was about noon when I heard the bell.

It sounded like bells I'd heard in St. Anna Bay and in the Schottegat. Small boats and tugs use them to tell the engineer to go slow or fast or put the engines in reverse.

For a moment, I thought I was dreaming.

Then I heard the bell again. And with it, the slow chugging of an engine. And voices! They were coming from east beach.

I ran down there. Yes, a small boat had come into the Devil's Mouth and was approaching our cay.

I yelled, "I'm here! I'm here!"

There was a shout from across the water. A man's voice. "We see you!"

I stood there on east beach, Stew Cat by my feet, looking in the direction of the sounds. I heard the bell again; then the engine went into reverse, the propeller thrashing. Someone yelled, "Jump, Scotty, the water's shallow."

The voice was American, I was certain.

The engine was now idling, and someone was coming toward me. I could hear him padding across the sand. I said, "Hello."

There was no answer from the man. I suppose he was just staring at me.

Then he yelled to someone on the boat, "My Lord, it's a naked boy. And a cat!"

The person on the boat yelled, "Anyone else?"

I called out, "No, just us."

I began to move toward the man on the beach.

He gasped. "Are you blind?"

I said, "Yes, sir."

In a funny voice, he asked, "Are you all right?"

"I'm fine now. You're here," I said.

He said, "Here, boy, I'll help you."

I said, "If you'll carry Stew Cat, you can just lead me to the boat."

After I had climbed aboard, I remembered Timothy's knife stuck in the palm tree. It was the only thing I wanted off the cay. The sailor who had carried Stew Cat went up the hill to get it while the other sailor asked me questions. When the first sailor came back from the hill, he said, "You wouldn't believe what's up there." I guess he was talking about our hut and the rain catchment. He should have seen the ones Timothy built.

I don't remember everything that happened in the next few hours but very soon I was helped up the gangway of a destroyer. On deck I was asked so many questions all at once that one man barked, "Stop badgering him. Give him food, medical care, and get him into a bunk."

A voice answered meekly, "Yes, sir, Cap'n."

Down in sick bay, the captain asked, "What's your name, son?"

"Phillip Enright. My father lives in Willemstad. He works for Royal Dutch Shell," I answered.

The captain told someone to get a priority radio message off to the naval commander at Willemstad and then asked, "How did you get on that little island?"

"Timothy and I drifted on to it after the *Hato* was sunk."

"Where's Timothy?" he asked.

I told the captain about Timothy and what had happened to us. I'm not sure the captain believed any of it, because he said quietly, "Son, get some sleep. The *Hato* was sunk way back in April."

I said, "Yes, sir, that's right," and then a doctor came in to check me over.

That night, after the ship had been in communication with Willemstad, the captain visited me again to tell me that his destroyer had been hunting a German submarine when the plane had spotted my black smoke and radioed back to the ship.

There was still disbelief in his voice when he said he'd checked all the charts and publications on the bridge; our cay was so small that the charts wouldn't even dignify it with a name. But Timothy had been right. It was tucked back up in the Devil's Mouth.

The next morning, we docked at the naval base in Cristóbal, Panama, and I was rushed to a hospital, although I really didn't think it was necessary. I was strong and healthy, the doctor on the destroyer had said.

My mother and father flew over from Willemstad in a special plane. It was minutes before they could say anything. They just held me, and I knew my mother was crying. She kept saying, "Phillip, I'm sorry, I'm so sorry."

The Navy had notified them that I was blind, so that it would not be a shock. And I knew I looked different. They'd brought a barber in to cut my hair, which had grown quite long.

We talked for a long time, Stew Cat on my bed, and I tried to tell them all about Timothy and the cay. But it was very difficult. They listened, of course, but

I had the feeling that neither of them really understood what had happened on our cay.

Four months later, in a hospital in New York, after many X rays and tests, I had the first of three operations. The piece of timber that had hit me the night the *Hato* went down had damaged some nerves. But after the third operation, when the bandages came off, I could see again. I would always have to wear glasses, but I could see. That was the important thing.

In early April, I returned to Willemstad with my mother, and we took up life where it had been left off the previous April. After I'd been officially reported lost at sea, she'd gone back to Curaçao to be with my father. She had changed in many ways. She had no thoughts of leaving the islands now.

I saw Henrik van Boven occasionally, but it wasn't the same as when we'd played the Dutch or the British. He seemed very young. So I spent a lot of time along St. Anna Bay, and at the Ruyterkade market talking to the black people. I liked the sound of their voices. Some of them had known old Timothy from Charlotte Amalie. I felt close to them.

At war's end, we moved away from Scharloo and Curaçao. My father's work was finished.

Since then, I've spent many hours looking at charts of the Caribbean. I've found Roncador, Rosalind, Quito Sueño, and Serranilla Banks; I've found Beacon Cay and North Cay, and the islands of Providencia and San Andrés. I've also found the Devil's Mouth.

Someday, I'll charter a schooner out of Panama and explore the Devil's Mouth. I hope to find the lonely little island where Timothy is buried.

Maybe I won't know it by sight, but when I go ashore and close my eyes, I'll know this was our own cay. I'll walk along cast beach and out to the reef. I'll go up the hill to the row of palm trees and stand by his grave.

I'll say, "Dis b'dat outrageous cay, eh, Timothy?"

Related Readings

CONTENTS

Sea Poems

by Langston Hughes

*The sights, sounds, and movements of
the sea inspired these poems by Langston
Hughes. As you read, see what parts of
them trigger memories of Timothy and
Phillip's adventure.*

Long Trip

The sea is a wilderness of waves,
A desert of water.
We dip and dive,
Rise and roll,
5   Hide and are hidden
On the sea.
  Day, night,
  Night, day,
The sea is a desert of waves,
10   A wilderness of water.

Sea Calm

How still,
How strangely still
The water is today.
It is not good
5   For water
To be so still that way.

Death of an Old Seaman

We buried him high on the windy hill,
But his soul went out to sea.
I know, for I heard, when all was still,
His sea-soul say to me:

5   Put no tombstone at my head,
For here I do not make my bed.
Strew no flowers on my grave,
I've gone back to the wind and wave.
Do not, do not weep for me,
10 For I am happy with my sea.

from Survive the Savage Sea

by Dougal Robertson

In The Cay, *German submarines sink the S.S.* Hato, *leaving Phillip, Timothy, and others adrift in the shark-infested waters of the Caribbean Sea. In a similar but real-life incident in 1972, killer whales in the Pacific Ocean attacked and sunk the schooner* Lucette *(nicknamed Lucy). Left adrift on a rubber raft towed by a nine-foot dinghy are Dougal Robinson; his wife Lyn; their 18-year-old son Douglas; their 12-year-old twin boys Neil and Sandy; and Robin Williams, a family friend. In these journal entries, Robertson describes their struggle for survival.*

First day

We sat on the salvaged pieces of flotsam lying on the raft floor, our faces a pale bilious color under the bright yellow canopy, and stared at each other, the shock of the last few minutes gradually seeping through to our consciousness. Neil, his teddy bears gone, sobbed in accompaniment to Sandy's hiccup cry, while Lyn repeated the Lord's Prayer, then, comforting them, sang the hymn "For Those in Peril on the Sea." Douglas and Robin watched at the doors of the canopy to retrieve any useful pieces of debris which might float within reach and gazed with dumb longing at the distant five-gallon water container, bobbing its polystyrene lightness ever further away from us in the steady trade wind. The dinghy *Ednamair* wallowed, swamped, nearby with a line attached to it from the raft, and our eyes traveled over and beyond to the heaving undulations of the horizon, already searching for a rescue ship even while knowing there would not be one. Our eyes traveled fruitlessly across the limitless waste of sea and sky, then once more ranged over the scattering debris. Of the killer whales which had so recently shattered our very existence, there was no sign. Lyn's sewing basket floated close and it was brought aboard followed by a couple of empty boxes, the canvas raft cover, and a plastic cup.

I leaned across to Neil and put my arm round him, "It's all right now, son, we're safe and the whales have gone." He looked at me reproachfully. "We're not crying cos we're frightened," he sobbed, "we're crying cos Lucy's gone." Lyn gazed at me over their heads, her eyes filling with tears. "Me too," she said, and after a moment added, "I suppose we'd better find out how we stand."

This was the question I had been dreading; feelings of guilt, that our present predicament was not only due to my unorthodox ideas on educating our children (there had been plenty of critics to object that I was needlessly jeopardizing the children's lives) but also that I had failed to foresee this type of disaster, now engulfed me, and this, added to the fact that we had lost almost everything we possessed as well as *Lucette,* depressed me to the depths of despair. How could I have been so foolish as to trust our lives to such an old schooner! Then I saw, once again, in my mind's eye that damage under the floorboards of *Lucette*. Not only had the frames withstood the impact of the blow, but the new garboard strake of inch-and-a-half pitchpine, fitted in Malta at the surveyor's recommendation, had been one of the hull planks which had been smashed inward. Her hull had taken a full minute to sink below the waves, but a modern boat, constructed with less regard to brute strength than *Lucette*, would have sustained much heavier damage and sunk even more quickly, with more terrible results.

I looked at Douglas; he had grown to manhood in our eighteen months at sea together; the twins, previously shy, introspective farm lads, had become interested in the different peoples we had met and their various ways of life, and were now keen to learn more; I tried to ease my conscience with the thought that they had derived much benefit from their voyage and that our sinking was as unforeseeable as an earthquake, or an airplane crash, or anything to ease my conscience.

We cleared a space on the floor and opened the survival kit, which was part of the raft's equipment, and was contained in a three foot-long polythene cylinder; slowly we took stock:

Vitamin fortified bread and glucose for ten men for two days.

Eighteen pints of water, eight flares (two parachute, six hand).

One bailer, two large fish-hooks, two small, one spinner and trace and a twenty-five-pound breaking strain fishing line.

A patent knife which would not puncture the raft (or anything else for that matter), a signal mirror, torch, first-aid box, two sea anchors, instruction book, bellows, and three paddles.

In addition to this there was the bag of a dozen onions which I had given to Sandy, to which Lyn had added a one-pound tin of biscuits and a bottle containing about half a pound of glucose sweets, ten oranges and six lemons. How long would this have to last us? As I looked around our meager stores my heart sank and it must have shown on my face for Lyn put her hand on mine; "We must get these boys to land," she said quietly. "If we do nothing else with our lives, we must get them to land!" I looked at her and nodded, "Of course, we'll make it!" The answer came from my heart but my head was telling me a different story. We were over two hundred miles downwind and downcurrent from the Galapagos Islands. To try to row the small dinghy into two hundred miles of rough ocean weather was an impossible journey even if it was tried by only two of us in an attempt to seek help for the others left behind in the raft. The fact that the current was against us as well only put the seal of hopelessness on the idea. There was no way back.

The Marquesas Islands lay two thousand eight hundred miles to the west but we had no compass or means of finding our position; if, by some miraculous feat of endurance, one of us made the distance the chances of striking an island were remote.

The coast of Central America, more than a thousand miles to the northeast, lay on the other side of the windless Doldrums, that dread area of calms and squalls which had inspired Coleridge's

> Water, water, everywhere,
> And all the boards did shrink;
> Water, water, everywhere,
> Nor any drop to drink.

I was a Master Mariner, I thought ruefully, not an ancient one, and could count on no ghostly crew to get me out of this dilemma! What were our chances if we followed the textbook answer, "Stay put and wait for rescue"? In the first place we wouldn't be missed for at least five weeks and if a search was made, where would they start looking in three thousand miles of ocean? In the second place the chance of seeing a passing vessel in this area was extremely remote and could be discounted completely, for of the two possible shipping routes from Panama to Tahiti and New Zealand, one lay four hundred miles to the south and the other three hundred miles to the north. Looking at the food, I estimated that six of us might live for ten days and since we could expect no rain in this area for at least six months, apart from an odd shower, our chances of survival beyond ten days were doubtful indeed. It seemed to me that we stood a very good chance of becoming one of Robin's statistics.

My struggle to reach a decision, gloomy whichever way I looked at it, showed on my face, and Lyn leaned forward. "Tell us how we stand," she said, looking around. "We want to know the truth." They all nodded. "What chance have we?" I could not tell them I thought they were going to die so I slowly spelled out the alternatives, and then suddenly I knew there was only one course open to us; we must sail with the trade winds to the Doldrums four hundred miles to the north. We stood a thin chance of reaching land but the only possible shipping route lay in that direction, our only possible chance of rain water in any quantity lay in that direction even if it was four hundred miles away, and our only possible chance of reaching land lay in that direction, however small that chance might be. We would work and fight for our lives at least; better than dying in idleness! "We must get these boys to land," Lyn had said. I felt the reality of the decision lifting the hopelessness from my shoulders and looked around; five pairs of eyes watched me as I spoke, Lyn once again with her arms around the twins. "We have no alternative," I said. . . .

During the days that followed, all of the crew wrote farewell letters to their loved ones on pieces of sail. They then placed their letters in a waterproof wrapping and tucked them into a pocket of the raft. By the seventh day, still 150 miles from the doldrums, the crew had only six pints of water left.

Seventh day

The windless night filled our ears with unaccustomed silence, and in the quiet of the calm swell the phosphorescent gleam of the large dorado, streaking from under the raft and leaping high into the air, to land in bursting showers of green glowing fire, was a display not often seen by men.

The foul dryness of our mouths aggravated the discomfort of our sleepless bodies as we tried to ease the agony of our thirst, twisting this way and that, then breathlessly we watched the gathering clouds obscure the stars and as dawn paled the eastern horizon, it began to rain, a heavy shower this time, with a steady downpour. Slowly the water in the pipe from the canopy ran clear and we filled our empty cans and spare plastic bags, our bellies and our mouths until we could not force down another drop. We lay with our faces turned to the sky and let the pure fresh water cleanse the salt from our beards and hair; suddenly everything had changed from the shadow of the specter of death to the joyful prospect of life, and all by a shower of rain. We would make the doldrums now! We lay uncaring, chewing strips of dorado and reveling in the absence of thirst, talking excitedly of good food and watching the bulging plastic bags swing lazily from the roof of the canopy. We had water!

Douglas, lazily watching the dispersing clouds, suddenly sat up with a start, pointing excitedly. "A ship! A ship! It's a ship!" We all crowded to the door of the raft, staring in the direction of his pointing finger; a cargo vessel of about six thousand tons was approaching us on a course that would bring her within three miles of us. I felt my heart pound against my ribs. "Get out the flares," I said hoarsely, "and pass them to me in the dinghy, they'll see us better from there."

Three miles was a fair distance, but on a dull day like this, against a background of rain they should see us easily. I clambered into the dinghy and Douglas passed me the rockets and hand flares; my hands trembled as I ripped open a parachute rocket flare and, with a mute appeal to the thing to fire, struck the igniter on the fuse. It spluttered and hissed, then roared off on a trajectory high above the raft, its pinkish magnesium flare slowly spiraling downward leaving a trail of smoke in the sky. They couldn't fail to see it. I waited a moment or two watching for the ship to alter course, then struck a hand flare, holding it high above my head. The blinding red light was hot to hold and I pointed it away from the wind to ease my hand, the red embers of the flare dropping into the dinghy; as it went out

I struck another, smoke from the first now a rising plume in the sky; surely they must see that. I waited a little, my hands trembling. "This chance might not come again," I said, anxious faces crowding the door of the raft, "I'm going to use our last rocket flare and one more hand flare." We watched tensely as the second rocket flare soared and spiraled its gleaming distress message high above us; desperately I struck the third hand flare and held it high, standing on the thwart and holding on to the mast. "Look, look, you bastards!" I shouted. "Set fire to the sail!" Lyn's voice. I stuck the flare to the sail but it only melted. The ship sailed on, slowly disappearing behind a rain shower, and when she reappeared her hull was half obscured by the horizon, five miles distant and disappearing fast. The time was eleven o'clock. My shoulders drooped. "We daren't use another," I said. "They won't see it now and we have to keep something for the next one." We had three hand flares left. Lyn smiled cheerfully. "It says in the instruction book that the first one probably wouldn't see us," she said slowly, "and I'd already told the twins not to expect anything." She gathered the twins to her, comfortingly. We stared at the dwindling speck on the horizon and felt so lonely that it hurt. . . .

Each night, the older members of the crew took turns bailing out the leaking raft and blowing air into its floatation chambers. By day, they kept a careful watch for the huge sharks that had become their constant companions. The crew managed to catch a large turtle to use for food. Everyone grew increasingly uncomfortable with boils, swellings of the skin caused by the irritation of continuous contact with sea water.

Fourteenth day

The beautiful starlit night shone sparkles of stars on the quiet swells of the now distant trade winds, and seemed to mock our feeble struggle for existence in the raft; to become one with the night would be so easy. We blew, and bailed the forward section continually, and when Sandy found the hole which leaked into the after section, surrounded by transparently thin fabric, I felt that this was the beginning of the end of the raft. I knew that it was unlikely that I would be able to plug this one, and yet if I left it, it would certainly split open in the next heavy sea. I made a plug and inserted it into the hole, tape ready to bind it if it held. The hole split across and water flooded into the after compartment; I rammed the plug home in disgust and stopped enough of the water to bail the compartment dry but the raft would now need constant bailing at both ends. Apart from discomfort, my only real opposition to abandoning the raft was because it would mean abandoning the shelter afforded by the canopy, so I decided to think of a way of fastening the canopy on the dinghy to give us continuing shelter from the sun if we had to abandon.

We had a sip of water for breakfast with no dried food to detract from its value, after which I crossed to the dinghy to try for a dorado. The heat of the sun's rays beat on my head like a club and my mouth, dry like lizard skin, felt full of my tongue; the slightest exertion left me breathless. I picked up the spear; the dorado were all deep down as if they knew I was looking for them. A bump at the stern of the raft attracted Sandy's attention. "Turtle!" he yelled. This one was much smaller than the first and with great care it was caught and passed through the raft—with Douglas guarding its beak, and the others its claws, from damaging the fabric—to me on the dinghy where I lifted it aboard without much trouble. I wrapped a piece of tape around the broken knife blade and made the incision into its throat. "Catch the blood," Lyn called from the raft. "It should be all right to drink a little." I held the plastic cup under the copious flow of blood, the cup filled quickly and I stuck another under as soon as it was full, then raising the full cup to my lips, tested it cautiously. It wasn't salty at all! I tilted the cup and drained it. "Good stuff!" I shouted. I felt as if I had just consumed the elixir of life. "Here, take this," and I passed the bailer full of blood, about a pint, into the raft for the others to drink. Lyn said afterward she had imagined that she would have to force it down us and the sight of me, draining the cup, my mustache dripping blood, was quite revolting. I don't know what I looked like, but it certainly tasted good, and as the others followed my example it seemed they thought so too. I passed another pint across and though some of this coagulated before it could be drunk, the jelly was cut up and the released serum collected and used as a gravy with the dried turtle and fish.

I set to cutting my way into the turtle much refreshed, and even with the broken knife, made faster work of it than the first one, both because it was smaller, and being younger the shell was not so tough; the fact that I now knew my way around inside a turtle helped a lot too.

The sky was serenely blue that afternoon and with our position worked out at 500 north, 250 miles west of Espinosa, we had arrived at the official limits of the doldrums. Was this, then, doldrums weather? Was "The Rime of the Ancient Mariner" right with its "Nor any drop to drink?" We had four tins of water left, one of them half sea water, and if any of the other three contained short measure, well, there might come another turtle. I looked around the raft at the remains of Robin and the Robertson family, water-wrinkled skin covered with salt-water boils and raw red patches of rash, lying in the bottom of the raft unmoving except to bail occasionally, and then only halfheartedly, for the water was cooling in the heat of the day; our bones showed clearly through our scanty flesh; we had become much thinner these last few days and our condition was deteriorating fast. The raft was killing us with its demands on our energy. Douglas looked across at me, "Do you think it'll rain tonight, Dad?" I looked at him and shrugged, looked at the sky, not a cloud. "I suppose it could do," I said. "Do you think it will?" he insisted. "For heaven's sake, Douglas, I'm not a prophet," I said testily. "We'll just have to wait it out." His eyes looked hopeless at the blue of the sea from the deep cavities under his brow; how could I comfort him when he knew as well as I that it might not rain for a week and that we'd be dead by then. I said, "Fresh turtle for tea, we can suck something out of that." We could live on turtles, maybe.

We took no water that evening, only a little for the twins. We talked of the dishes we'd like to eat in the gathering twilight and I chose fresh fruit salad and ice cream; Lyn, a tin of apricots; Robin, strawberries and ice cream with milk; Douglas, the same as me; Neil, chocolate chip ice cream; Sandy, fresh fruit, ice cream and milk—gallons of ice-cool milk. Later that night as I took the watch over from Douglas, he described in detail the dish he had dreamed up during his watch. "You take a honeydew melon," he said. "Cut the top off and take out the seeds; that's the dish. Chill it and drop a knob of ice cream in, then pile in strawberries, raspberries, pieces of apple, pear, orange, peach and grapefruit, the sweet sort, then cherries and grapes until the melon is full; pour a lemon syrup over it and decorate it with chips of chocolate and nuts. Then," he said with a dreamy expression on his face, "you eat it!" "I'll have one too," I said, taking the bailer from his boil-covered hand; I looked at the sky; to the northeast a faint film of cirrostratus cloud dimmed the stars, "You know, I think it might rain by morning." I could feel him relax in the darkness; his voice came slowly, "I'll be all right if it doesn't, Dad," he said.

I started to bail mechanically. We would have to abandon the raft, soon, I thought, and that meant ditching all the unnecessary stuff overboard; in the dinghy there was only room for food, water, flares and us. We'd start to sort things out in the morning.

Fifteenth day

. . . It rained at dawn, beautiful, gorgeous rain. We saved three and a half gallons and drank our fill besides; the wind, from the south, freshened a little and as the weather cleared we lay back and enjoyed the sensation of being without thirst, bailing and blowing unheeded for the moment. We talked of the ship that didn't see us, for that had happened after the last rain, and argued whether it would have seen us better if it had been night time. The twins were talking when Douglas, on watch, his voice desperate with dismay, called, "Dad, the dinghy's gone!" I was across the raft in an instant. I looked at the broken end of wire trailing in the water, the broken line beside it. The dinghy was sixty yards away, sailing still and our lives were sailing away with it; I was the fastest swimmer, no time for good-bys, to hell with sharks; the thoughts ran through my head as I was diving through the door, my arms flailing into a racing crawl even as I hit the water. I heard Lyn cry out but there was no time for talk. Could I swim faster than the dinghy could sail, that was the point; I glanced at it as I lifted my head to breathe, the sail had collapsed as the dinghy yawed, I moved my arms faster, kicked harder, would the sharks let me, that was another point; my belly crawled as I thought of the sharks, my arms moved faster still; I glanced again, only thirty yards to go but she was sailing again, I felt no fatigue, no cramped muscles, my body felt like a machine as I thrashed my way through the sea only one thought now in mind, the dinghy or us. Then I was there; with a quick heave I flipped over the stern of the dinghy to safety, reached up and tore down the sail before my knees buckled and I lay across the thwart trembling and gasping for breath, my heart pounding like a hammer. I lifted my arm and waved to the raft, now two hundred yards away, then slowly I untied the paddle from the sail and paddled back to the raft; it took nearly half an hour. The long shapes of two sharks circled curiously twenty feet down; they must have had breakfast.

Lyn had been sitting against the central thwart

trying to rest after her watch and the following is her account of what happened in the raft after Douglas shouted, "Dad, the dinghy's gone."

I saw Dougal's body hurtle past me as he dived into the sea. The silence was broken by the cry of "Shark" from Douglas, followed by a despairing shriek from Neil, "Daddy! Daddy!" We all crowded to see past Douglas blocking the doorway. Dougal was cutting through the water faster than *Ednamair* was sailing and could not have kept up such a speed for more than a few minutes. The shark was close behind him to his right and his feet were threshing the water in a racing crawl. "I can't see him," I said, "he's gone." The raft had slewed around in the swell and we had lost sight of him. "Don't panic! Don't panic!" Robin shouted. Then Douglas cried, "He's done it! He's made it!" "Good old Dad," this from Sandy. Only Douglas could see him now and he gave us a running commentary. "He's taking the sail down now, it's down, he's getting the paddle off the sail." Douglas craned his neck to see as the raft slewed around more, and we scrambled over the thwart to the aft compartment to look through the back door. There, miraculously, we saw him, the dinghy like a cockleshell on the crest of a wave with Dougal paddling furiously, first one side then the other with such a look of concentration and determination on his haggard face. Relief flooded through me and I heard myself singing "Somewhere My Love," that wonderful song from *Dr. Zhivago.* It was a long time before he reached us and as he fell through the doorway into the bottom of the raft, his face gray with exhaustion, I pressed the sipper jar to his lips. He shook his head but I made him drink, then I put a piece of glucose in his mouth, cradling his head in my arms until his strength returned, and shuddering as I thought of how lonely and desperate we had felt cut off from our only hope for survival, *Ednamair* and my beloved Dougal. . . .

On the 17th day, the family finally deserted the sinking raft for the dinghy, where they then had to endure crowded sleeping conditions. On the 29th day, a fierce battle took place between Dougal and a pesky shark. Dougal said: "We had turned the tables on our most feared enemy; sharks would not eat Robertsons, Robertsons would eat sharks!"

In quieter moments, the family sang songs and told stories. They also played games and discussed Dougal's Kitchen, a fantasy restaurant where each member imagined a wonderful menu.

Thirty-eighth day

. . . I chopped up some dried turtle meat for tea, and Lyn put it with a little wet fish to soak in meat juice. She spread the dry sheets for the twins under the canopy, then prepared their "little supper" as we started to talk of Dougal's Kitchen and if it should have a wine license. As we pondered the delights of Gaelic coffee, my eye, looking past the sail, caught sight of something that wasn't sea. I stopped talking and stared; the others all looked at me. "A ship," I said. "There's a ship and it's coming toward us!" I could hardly believe it but it seemed solid enough. "Keep still now!" In the sudden surge of excitement, everyone wanted to see. "Trim her! We mustn't capsize now!" All sank back to their places.

I felt my voice tremble as I told them that I was going to stand on the thwart and hold a flare above the sail. They trimmed the dinghy as I stood on the thwart. "Right, hand me a flare, and remember what happened with the last ship we saw!" They suddenly fell silent in memory of that terrible despondency when our signals had been unnoticed. "O God!" prayed Lyn, "please let them see us." I could see the ship quite clearly now, a Japanese tuna fisher. Her gray and white paint stood out clearly against the dark cross swell. "Like a great white bird," Lyn said to the twins, and she would pass within about a mile of us at her nearest approach. I relayed the information as they listened excitedly, the tension of not knowing, of imminent rescue, building like a tangible, touchable, unbearable unreality around me. My eye caught the outlines of two large sharks, a hundred yards to starboard. "Watch the trim," I warned. "We have two maneating sharks waiting if we capsize!" Then, "I'm going to light the flare now, have the torch ready in case it doesn't work."

I ripped the caps off, pulled out the striker and struck the primer. The flare smoked then sparked into life, the red glare illuminating *Ednamair* and the sea around us in the twilight. I could feel my index finger roasting under the heat of the flare and waved it to and fro to escape the searing heat radiating outward in the calm air; then unable to bear the heat any longer, I dropped my arm, nearly scorching Lyn's face, and threw the flare high in the air. It curved in a brilliant arc and dropped into the sea. "Hand me another, I think she's altered course!" My voice was hoarse with pain and excitement and I felt sick with apprehension that it might only be the ship corkscrewing in the swell, for she had made no signal that she had seen us. The second flare didn't work. I cursed it in frustrated anguish as the priming substance chipped off instead of lighting. "The torch!" I shouted, but it wasn't needed, she had seen us, and was coming toward us.

I flopped down on the thwart. "Our ordeal is over," I said quietly. Lyn and the twins were crying with happiness; Douglas, with tears of joy in his eyes, hugged his mother. Robin laughed and cried at the same time, slapped me on the back and shouted "Wonderful! We've done it. Oh! Wonderful!" I put my arms about Lyn feeling the tears stinging my own eyes: "We'll get these boys to land after all." As we shared our happiness and watched the fishing boat close with us, death could have taken me quite easily just then, for I knew that I would never experience another such pinnacle of contentment.

The Shark

by John Ciardi

Timothy warns Phillip twice about the
sharks swimming around their life raft.
Consider this poem your first warning.

My dear, let me tell you about the shark.
Though his eyes are bright, his thought
    is dark.
He's quiet—that speaks well of him.
So does the fact that he can swim.
5   But though he swims without a sound,
Wherever he swims he looks around
With those two bright eyes and that one
    dark thought.
He has only one but he thinks it a lot.
And the thought he thinks but can never
    complete
10   Is his long dark thought of something
    to eat.
Most anything does. And I have to add
That when he eats his manners are bad.
He's a gulper, a ripper, a snatcher, a grabber.
Yes, his manners are drab. But his thought is
    drabber.
15   That one dark thought he can never
    complete
Of something—anything—somehow to eat.

Be careful where you swim, my sweet.

from The Killer Storms

by Gary Jennings

On a hot day in July, churning waves around the cay make sharp sounds like rifle shots, warning Timothy that a terrible storm is coming. This nonfiction excerpt gives information about hurricanes and typhoons. Discover how the enormous power of these storms has changed the course of history.

HURAKÁN

The islands known today as the West Indies are probably the nearest thing to paradise found on this earth.

The first explorers to find them—before history began—were the brown-skinned tribes called Taíno, Lucayo, and Igneri, who originally lived along the northern coasts of the South American continent. These were gentle people, and their life on the mainland had been made intolerable by more warlike neighbors, the Caribs, who continually preyed upon them. Preferring flight to fight, the beleaguered people ventured out to sea in canoes— one party after another over the years—and beyond the horizon they found a haven in these islands. . . .

The newcomers were thankful for this paradise they'd found, and they were dutiful about saying "thank you" to the various gods they believed responsible for their good luck. Like most primitive peoples, these tribesmen did not recognize one single, all-powerful god, but saw a separate spirit in every different aspect of nature. There might be one god of flowers, another of trees, another of fruits, a god of the sun, and a god of the sea. The islanders thanked them all for the bounty they had bestowed—and continued to pray and offer sacrifices so the gods would go on giving their blessings.

For example, even in paradise some rain must fall. When the islands began to be parched after a season of uninterrupted sunshine, the people would appeal to their rain god, and in due course would come the refreshing showers. Sometimes, though, these came with thunder and lightning, not so welcome as the simple rain. So the people had a separate storm god, too, and to him they prayed *not* to send his blessings.

Nevertheless, almost every year there came at least one storm that was worse than all the other storms put together. Its black clouds and deluge of rain rode a wind like a battering-ram, a wind that no man, no palm-leaf hut, and sometimes not even the sturdiest trees could stand against. The most awful thing about this particular storm was that it seldom struck just once and then moved on. Often it was two disasters rolled into one.

Its first murderous onslaught might last for hours or a day or more, then there would be a pause as if the storm was gathering its breath. But in a matter of minutes, or an hour, or a few hours at the most, the storm would strike again just as fiercely as before— only now from the opposite direction. The few huts that had stood fast during the storm's first pass could seldom survive this second smashing blow from their other flank.

The islanders already had their rain god to thank for life-giving showers. And they had their storm god to blame for thunderbolts and cloudbursts. But this one distinctive kind of storm was so exceptionally devastating that they thought it simply must have a separate god of its own, and him they beseeched with their most heartfelt fervor *please* to stay away.

To this dread god the islanders gave the name of Hurakán.

HURRICANE!

Today we know that this killer storm is not really the work of any bad-tempered god. We know that it is simply a vast, churning circle of winds—like a merry-go-round gone wild—roaring around a central area (the "eye") that is comparatively calm and still. Like a merry-go-round mounted on a truck, the storm travels in a forward direction at the same time that it is fiercely whirling. First the leading edge of the spinning storm sweeps over a ground area, then the calm eye, then the storm's trailing edge. Thus, although the storm essentially consists of just one circling wind, it *does* strike twice from opposite directions.

The storm is not really a "killer" in the sense that it destroys deliberately or has any ill will of its own. The storm develops from the natural interactions of heat, air, moisture, and the rotation of the earth, and so it is no more a monstrosity than sunshine or the seasons. But it is the most powerful and destructive force that has ever been unleashed on our world. Compared to the energy let loose in just one such storm, other natural upheavals like volcanoes and earthquakes, or man-made devastations like a hydrogen-bomb explosion, are comparative pipsqueaks.

So, although this kind of weather disturbance is an entirely natural phenomenon of nature, "killer storm" remains an accurate epithet for it.

The killer storm still bedevils us, just as it did the earliest inhabitants of the West Indies, and we might say that the dread god does, too, since our word "hurricane" derives from his name. *Hurakán* was one of the first native words that the white man learned when he arrived in the New World, because the storm was the first and worst danger he encountered here.

It's a minor miracle that the earliest and most famous of all the white explorers ever arrived safely in these islands, or got safely back to Europe to announce his discovery. It was August, the very peak of the "hurricane season," when Christopher Columbus set out from Spain on his initial voyage in 1492, and he set his course for that part of the Atlantic Ocean where the hurricanes blow the worst. Of course, Columbus did not know that hurricanes existed. But it may be that he had a brush with one of these mighty storms without even realizing it.

At one point in mid-ocean, his three tiny ships were tossed and rocked by a heavy sea swell. These waves were something new in the sailors' experience, because there was no accompanying high wind to account for them. Almost certainly they were the evidence of a hurricane raging somewhere far over the horizon, because such a storm can send billows surging thousands of miles across the sea.

These oddly windless waves were a puzzle, but no hazard, and eventually the explorers made landfall in those islands known today as the Bahamas. During the remainder of that first exploration of the New World, the adventurers never felt any other touch of a hurricane. On the return trip to Spain, early in 1493, they endured no storm worse than the Atlantic's winter gales.

During his later voyages to the West Indies, Columbus did encounter full-blown hurricanes, and confessed his terror of them. After one violent storm had sunk three of his ships, he remarked that, except for his desire to serve God and king—by finding new lands in which to plant the Christian religion and the flag of Spain—*nothing* would induce him to expose himself to such dangers as the wrath of the hurricane.

Other seafarers fanning out from Europe into other alien seas also found devastating storms and, if they survived, they learned the native names for them. Around the Gulf of Arabia, for instance, the most dreaded storm was the *asifa-t.* The fiercest storm of the North Pacific was known to the Chinese as the *ty-fung,* meaning "great wind" (the European sailors found it easier to say "tuffoon" or "typhoon"). In the Philippine Islands the same storm was called the *baguio,* and in Japan the *reppu.* The first white settlers of Australia copied a native word and called the worst of their coastal storms the "willy-willy." On the other side of the Pacific, along the western seaboard of Mexico and Central America, the Spanish colonists called the storm the *cordonazo.*

Although these great storms have long had different names, and are found in widely scattered areas, all of them are really the same kind of weather disturbance—identical to the hurricane—with only minor variations according to the part of the world that it occurs in. Since the people of each area still call "their" storm by its local name, a single such storm may be variously described as a *baguio*, a *ty-fung* and a *reppu*, as it roars past the Philippines, the China coast and then the islands of Japan. However, most professional weather forecasters today use only two of the old-time names. If the storm takes place anywhere in the western hemisphere, it is called a hurricane; in the Far East it's a typhoon.

By whatever name it is known, this worst of all the earth's storms can be more than an immediate disaster in one particular locality; it can have wide-ranging effects on people and events far removed from its area of activity. We realize, now, that the success of Columbus' first expedition, and his discovery of the New World, resulted from the absence of any interfering hurricane. But more often the *presence* of such a storm has drastically changed the course of human history.

During the great Age of Exploration that followed Columbus' trail-blazing voyages, the far-wandering seafarers brought back to Europe horrendous tales of the storms they had survived in foreign seas, and made words like "typhoon" and "willy-willy" familiar. But the storm and the name that became best known was "hurricane"—simply because it was encountered the most often by European sailors.

With the opening up of the New World, many more ships went there than to any other corner of the earth. Spanish, Portuguese, French, Dutch, and English explorers scouted the coasts of both North and South America. The Spanish conquistadors forged inland, wresting vast territories from the natives. Treasure-hunters came, and missionaries bringing Christianity. Colonists came to settle and to work the land. Pirates came, to prey on the merchant ships and to plunder the young port cities. For some two centuries after Columbus, most of this sea traffic and land settlement was concentrated among the islands of the West Indies and around the Gulf of Mexico coast from Yucatán to Florida. This is the area of the worst hurricanes. . . .

It is understandable that history could have been so often affected by the interference of hurricanes when the world's exploration, settlement, commerce, and warfare depended so heavily on wooden ships under canvas sails. But the same storms have equally affected the course of history in more modern times, when ships began to be built of sturdy metal and powered with mechanical engines.

In 1889, when the navy of every leading nation consisted of steam-driven, armor-plated warships, a Pacific typhoon proved that such dreadnaughts were still no more than toys compared to its own destructive power. At the same time, this storm stopped a war in the making.

In the 1880s Germany was attempting to expand its empire by annexing new colonies; one of the places Germany wanted was the island group of Samoa in the South Pacific, strategically situated midway between Hawaii and Australia. The Samoans were unwilling to give up their independence, so Germany sent three warships into the islands' harbor of Apia as a threatening "show of force." When the Samoans still refused to yield, the warships bombarded a native village on shore.

Because there were numerous Americans living in Samoa, the United States dispatched three warships of its own to protect its citizens' lives and property. On March 16, 1889, the American and German naval squadrons confronted each other in Apia harbor. If either side had made the slightest bellicose move at that point, the "Open fire!" order would have been given, and the resulting battle could only have led to a full-scale war between Germany and the United States. However, before any overt actions were made by the combatants, a typhoon crashed down on the islands.

All six of the ships were hurled onto the island reefs, some of them dashed to pieces against the rocks, others stranded helplessly, still others sunk in the tumult of waters—and 150 of the sailors lost their lives. The storm proved to be a common enemy for the Germans and the Americans—and the Samoan islanders as well—so all three factions united as allies to struggle against it. German crewmen washed overboard were plucked from the sea by American lifeboats. German ships threw towlines to haul American vessels off the murderous reefs. The Samoan villagers rescued the castaways of both navies who tumbled ashore half-drowned in the thundering breakers.

Thanks to the typhoon, the almost-war was ended before it began. Instead of deciding Samoa's future at gunpoint, Germany and the United States settled it peaceably—over a conference table later that year—when they and other major world powers agreed that the island group was to remain independent under its own rulers, a neutral territory not to be claimed by any other nation.

One other result of the Samoa incident was the United States' increasing realization that it had "come of age" as a major power—that it now ranked beside the most respected nations of the Old World, and shared their responsibility for helping keep the peace in all parts of the planet. To do its part in curbing warlike aggressors, the United States needed a larger navy, so it began to build new fighting ships. In short, that historic storm contributed to the founding of the modern United States Navy.

That proud navy has not endured many defeats since its formation. One of the few really terrible trouncings it ever suffered was inflicted by still another typhoon. It happened in December of 1944, toward the end of World War II, when the Allied forces were in the process of retaking the Philippine Islands from the Japanese troops who had invaded them early in the war. The Allies had secured possession of several of the smaller southern islands. Now they planned to mount their major assault on the Philippines' main island of Luzon, and in preparation for the landing the Allies were "softening up" the Japanese occupation forces with an intensive air and artillery bombardment by the U.S. Navy's Third Fleet.

After one of its strikes against the Japanese fortifications on Luzon, the Third Fleet withdrew a few hundred miles into the open ocean to rendezvous with tanker ships and refuel for the next foray. But the fleet was caught in mid-Pacific, in the middle of the fueling procedure, by a typhoon that had blown up unnoticed by the Navy weathermen.

Taken by surprise, with many of the ships still too low on fuel to outrun the storm, the fleet milled about in confusion. First it tried to maintain some kind of orderly formation, so that any vessel in distress would have help close at hand. When it became apparent that this tactic only added the danger of ships' ramming into each other, the fleet separated, every vessel for itself, to ride out the storm as best it might.

Three destroyers sank without a trace. Thirteen

craft were so severely damaged that they could barely limp back to an Allied port for repairs. Eight other vessels suffered less crippling injuries. The fleet's aircraft carriers lost 146 of their warplanes, either washed off the flight decks or battered into junk. The various ships lost a total of 763 men, either killed on board or vanished overside never to be seen again, and eighty other men were seriously injured.

All in all, it was a worse "defeat" than the Japanese Navy had been able to inflict on the U.S. Navy during the long campaign of fighting for the Philippines. It was fully three weeks before the Third Fleet was capable of combat again—three weeks during which further sea strikes against the Japanese in the Philippines had to be suspended—and without the bombardments the planned invasion of Luzon had to be postponed until early January of 1945.

The typhoon did not, of course, lose the war for the Allies. But the 1944 storm *did* temporarily bring to a standstill the world's most modern and efficient fighting machine. . . . For all our modern technology, we still cannot build a vessel for sea or air travel that can be *guaranteed* secure against the fury of a typhoon or hurricane. So long as so much of our civilization depends on transport and communication across the skies and oceans, the course of world history will still be steered occasionally by the capricious whims of the killer storm.

From the shores of what used to be the New World, America's astronauts are now looking upward at still newer worlds to conquer. Of this new breed of explorers the first advance scouts have already set foot on the moon. It will not be long before other adventurers make landfall on Mars.

After that, there are the other planets, other solar systems, the whole limitless reach of the universe to explore.

The techniques, skills, complex equipment, and sheer human bravery required for space travel make Columbus' crossing of the Atlantic seem simple. But, for all its fantastic differences, space exploration begins—just as did Columbus' voyage—with the setting-sail from an earthly harbor. And one of the hazards outside that harbor, a hazard that even a space ship must take into account, is the killer storm.

One "port of departure" for American space ships has been Cape Kennedy, Florida [now called Cape Canaveral], well inside hurricane territory. . . . On several occasions, the presence or likelihood of a hurricane in the vicinity has caused postponement of a vehicle's launching, because the storm threatened either the liftoff or the vehicle's recovery after splashdown.

Colin's Island

by Lynn Joseph

Because the cay is tucked in among other small islands and is surrounded by banks of sharp coral, Phillip and Timothy wonder if a boat could ever come close enough to discover them. In this tale, a storyteller from the Caribbean island of Trinidad describes an island so mysterious and so special that she hopes its location is kept secret.

Tantie's stories are so good that I started writing them down. I wanted to make sure I remember the way she tell it. When I told her what I was doing, she just waved her hand and said, "By your mouth or on de paper, it don't matter as long as you pass them on. But a good storyteller stirs up de old words to make new soup."

One time, though, Tantie told me and my cousins a strange story about a mysterious island that rose out of the sea, and she said I shouldn't write it down.

It was the middle of August holidays, and the days were slow and sticky. It was rainy season, but no rain had fallen in two weeks. The rivers had dried into clumps of dirt and the frogs had left home. The grass was brown and sad. The street dogs and cats lay under the cars all day long hiding from the hot, waxy sun. Even the beach and tennis people closed their doors on August. Only us children were running around enjoying the days off from school like always.

We pitched marbles under the cherry tree. We held bike obstacle races around empty Coke bottles. We climbed the hills and mashed down trails with our dull cutlasses. We didn't care that everyone was complaining about the unusual weather.

Then one day, Tantie came by my house to visit with Mama. She was looking all fancied up, and she had a big grip with her.

"You going on a trip, Tantie?" I asked.

Tantie nodded.

"Where?" Avril asked.

Tantie put down her grip and took off her flower hat. "I going down south to Cedros, chile," said Tantie. "For a nice, quiet seaside holiday. All yuh ever heard of Cedros?"

Me and Avril looked at each other and at Susan, Cedric, and Gerard. I wasn't too sure where Cedros was, and I could tell they weren't either.

"No, Tantie," we muttered, kind of shameful.

"Good," Tantie said, with a big smile. "I hope them others don't know 'bout it either."

"Who is them others?" I asked.

"People with big, big eyes," said Tantie. She looked at each of us one by one, as if checking to see if any of us was one of them.

Tantie took off her dress shoes and put on her house slippers. Then she sat down on a brown hassock and called for my mama. "Sylvie," she said, "give me some coconut to grate while I tell these children about Cedros."

Mama handed Tantie a big bowl and some coconut chunks for grating. I thought Tantie would start telling a story right then, but instead she looked at me and said, "Don't write this one down, Amber. It could cause all kind of bacchanal."

"How?" I asked.

Tantie said, "When words written down neat neat and just so, is like people believe de story more. But this story I telling you could cause people to believe too much. Although this story true, we don't want people to think so."

Well, I wasn't sure what Tantie was talking about but I said okay. Then Tantie began her story.

"One rainy season, a long time ago, de rain forget to fall, just like this year. De rivers dried up and all de fish moved out to de sea. De sky was bright blue with no clouds. And de sun shine hot hot like a fire we couldn't put out. De fruits dried up on de tree branches like brown lumps. De whole island looked like it needed a cool, wet hug. And everybody wished for rain.

"'If we only had some rain, we would never waste another drop,' de people said.

"'If we only had some rain, we would be nice to each other all de time,' they said.

"'If we only had some rain, we would be de happiest people in de world,' they said.

"But they didn't have any rain. So everyone quarreled about water.

"'Why your car clean so?' a man asked his neighbor.

"'My car ain't as clean as your hair,' said de neighbor. 'I en know about you but we en have extra water for no fancy hair washing.'

"'My hair! What about them white, white shoes you wearing there? I know is not spit you spit to get them so clean. Must be water you using up to walk so la-de-da.'

"But one boy needed de rain more than anyone else. His granny was dying in Cedros, in a tiny house by de sea, down at de southern tip of de island. All Granny wanted before she said good-bye to de world was to see some flowers.

"'But all de flowers are dead, Granny,' cried her grandson, Colin.

"Granny shook her head. 'There must be flowers somewhere. I have faith.'"

"Tantie," Avril interrupted. "You mean there wasn't a flower anywhere? In de whole island?"

Tantie nodded. "Yup," she said. "De place was dry like a monkey's eye at an alligator funeral.

"Anyway," Tantie continued, "Colin searched all over for flowers. He even went up to de big city, San Fernando, to de shops that sold flowers. But no one had any. Colin prayed for rain, so flowers would grow. But nothing happened. And each day he had to tell Granny, 'No flowers.'

"And she'd say, 'Yet.'

"One day, Colin sat on a large rock looking at de sun going down into de sea. Gold and orange sparkles flitted up from de water like mermaids' fingers reaching for de sky. Then darkness swooped down and lifted de sea-jewels, scattering them across de sky.

"Colin didn't have de energy to get up and go back to Granny's house without her flowers. 'O sea,' he said desperately, 'you are so wet and full of treasures, please give me a flower for my granny.'

"Colin's words floated over de sea. De waves hitting de rocks drowned him out. 'O sea,' Colin shouted, 'please share your treasures with me and I'll do anything you ask.'

"This time Colin's words did not float over de waves. They seemed to sink farther and farther down until they echoed with each wave hitting de rocks. De waves got blacker and wilder. Colin looked at them sadly, then trudged home.

"When Colin got to Granny's house, he thought he heard his name being whispered in de still trees. He looked around but everything was blackness. He peeped into Granny's room. And he stood stock still like de trees outside. Because all around Granny's bed were flowers. Red flowers, yellow ones, pink, purple, orange. And in de center was a big, beautiful sea-blue flower.

"'Look, Colin,' Granny whispered. 'My flowers came.'

"Colin stared at de happy flowers in de room. Then there was a loud noise like de sky had cracked open. And at last come de sound of rain. Heavy, wet, wonderful raindrops. Colin and Granny looked in each other's eyes and knew their prayers were answered. Colin went to bed with de sound of rain like a hand patting his head."

"Where de flowers come from, Tantie?" Susan asked, her eyes big and round.

Tantie shrugged. "Some things we don't wonder about too much because we go never find de answer."

"But, Tantie, you think Colin knew where de flowers came from?" I asked.

"No," said Tantie, "but I en finish de story yet.

"De next morning, Colin woke early. De rain hadn't stopped. De drops tapped on his window, calling to him.

"Colin got up and opened de window. There sitting smack dab in de middle of de sea, straight out from de beach in front of Granny's home, was a small, glistening, black island.

"Colin squeezed his eyes shut tightly and opened

them again. De island was still there, sparkling in de rain.

"'Oh my gosh,' said Colin. He pulled on his swim trunks and ran outside to de beach. He didn't even think about being scared. He just dove between de waves and swam straight for de island.

"As he pulled himself up onto de island, Colin understood why it was black and shining in de rain. Instead of dirt or sand, de island was covered in thick, black oil. Streams of oil flowed across it into black pools.

"Colin looked around slowly. He swished his hand through de oil. Then he tore a strip of cloth from his shorts and found a stick to tie it to. Colin planted his homemade flag in de thickest clump of oil he could find. De flag waved in de first cool breeze of de season. 'Colin's Island,' he said softly.

"De rain fell and fell on Colin and on de island. Colin could see de people on de mainland busy collecting rainwater in buckets and barrels. Nobody seemed to notice de island. That was fine with Colin.

"He sat and thought. De sea must have answered my wish for treasure. It helped bring de flowers and de rain, and, now this island. But what does it want from me?

"Colin looked down at his oil-covered legs and feet. He looked at de sea sitting quiet and blue except for de *plip plop* of raindrops striking de surface. He looked at de island—small, perfect, and wrapped in black glory.

"All day and night, Colin sat on his island feeling de wonderful rain fall on his head and shoulders. He felt he must wait for something, but he didn't know what. Then as de sky cleared, Colin's thoughts played out like a magical painting across de sky. And he saw all that would soon happen. People would come to his island. They would fight over de lovely dark oil. Strangers from other lands would come to gather up his oil and plunge huge machines into his quiet, blue sea to find more oil. De fish would die and lie rotting on de beach. The turtles would drown in de choked waters. He would not be able to swim at Cedros anymore. Or walk on de beach because his feet would stick to de tar-covered sand.

"Colin began to cry. His tears mixed with de oil. 'Go away,' he cried to his tiny island. 'Go away.'

"Then Colin dove into de sea and swam back to Granny's house. He fell asleep as de sun began to rise.

"When he woke up, de sun was high in de sky, daring de islanders to wish for more rain. Colin looked out his window. His island was gone! There was no shiny black anything, only blue, blue water all around.

"'It's gone,' he cried. 'Granny, it's gone.'

"But Granny shook her head. 'What you talking 'bout, boy?'

"'De island that rose out de sea yesterday—it's gone,' said Colin, happily.

"'Colin, stop that nonsense,' said Granny. 'I been looking out this window all day yesterday at de rain. Ain't no island rise out de sea here.'

"Colin heard de same thing all day. It was as if he had dreamed de island. De villagers laughed at him when he mentioned it.

"'You been drinking too much rainwater, boy,' they said.

"'No, no, his throat was so parched, it affect his brain,' they said.

"'So, what your little island like, Colin? You go be

prime minister and all?' They laughed at him.

"But Colin didn't say anything. He went back to Granny's house and sat on his bed. He wondered if he was going crazy. De island had been so real to him.

"Then Colin saw it. Lying on de floor in a corner was de pair of swim trunks from yesterday. It was covered in black oil. Colin smiled. And he went to bury de swim trunks deep in de backyard. He would never tell a soul about his oil discovery. Colin's mysterious island would be his own forever.

"And after his granny died, surrounded by rainbows of beautiful flowers, Colin spent many years walking on de clean Cedros sand and swimming in de clear blue sea."

Tantie handed us each a small piece of coconut to chew on. She dusted off some coconut from her lap. The story was finished. But neither me, nor Avril, Cedric, Susan, nor Gerard moved. I was thinking about the story.

Finally, I said, "Tantie, is a lot of questions I have about that story. Did Colin figure out what de sea wanted from him?"

"Well, Amber," said Tantie. "You could decide that for yourself. Some stories are like that. It go be different for each person. That's another reason why we don't write them down. Because then it's only one way."

Avril spoke up. "I think de sea was giving Colin a present in de small oil island. I mean, Colin did ask for some treasure. But Colin didn't want de sea's gift, right, Tantie?"

"What do you think?" Tantie asked.

Avril sucked on his coconut and was quiet. Tantie looked at me.

"I think Colin felt he had enough gifts from de sea already," I said. "De fish and de clean beach and de clear blue water for him to swim in. He didn't need an oil island too."

"Yeah, but Colin could have been rich," said Cedric.

"Depends on how you measure your riches," said Tantie.

Cedric looked at her, puzzled.

"Tantie," I said, "I think de sea wasn't expecting anything back from Colin. It was just giving him gifts. And letting him choose which gifts he wanted to keep forever."

Tantie didn't answer, but I could see a look in her eye that was like a smile. Then she waved her hands at us. "All yuh remember de story, but no writing it down, Amber."

A long time after Tantie told this story, a big announcement came over the Trinidad television. Oil had been discovered off Cedros Point. A big foreign oil company was coming to set up oil rigs and do some drilling. The whole island was buzzing with the talk of oil and riches.

Tantie came over that night, her head hanging low and her mouth set grim grim.

"Amber," she said, "they done opened their big, big eyes and found Colin's island. We go take one gift from de sea and mash up all de rest, just like Colin saw would happen. You might as well write down that story now. We reach de ending."

So I wrote it down. But Tantie's right. Sometimes it best not to write a story down neat neat and just so. Because then the ending can't change, and people might believe it too much.

Acknowledgments

Continued from page ii

Houghton Mifflin Company: "Colin's Island," from *The Mermaid's Twin Sister: More Stories From Trinidad* by Lynn Joseph. Text copyright © 1994 by Lynn Joseph. Reprinted by permission of Clarion Books/Houghton Mifflin Company. All rights reserved.